STOP WRECKING MY HOME

how to come out of a
broken marriage in one piece

Lauren McKinley

Cover Design by Kurtis Schureman, Caveman Crayon Design Studio

Manufactured in the United States of America

ISBN-13: 978-1539129554

ISBN-10: 1539129551

Stop Wrecking My Home, contains essays previously published on hersoulrepair.com as well as new material.

To the ones who checked on me by the hour,
making sure my broken heart
and daughter were doing okay.

To my cowboy,
who is God's greatest gift to my heart.

To my sweetie girl,
who I'd go through it all again for.
You are my brightest of all silver lining.

CONTENTS

1. HUSBAND, HOUSE & BABY

Existing for feelings is a terribly seductive and tormented road, one I wouldn't wish on anyone. The emotionally driven existence is one of shallow, fleeting moments. Moments that will only lead down deceitful paths. The advice to follow your heart makes me cringe. This favorite phrase takes the moral compass in all of us and crushes it. I have sadly witnessed this feelings-led path firsthand in the life of the man I was once married to, the father of my daughter. I will address him as Baby Daddy (BD) in this story, as it is the most respectful label for the content that follows. By chapter two, you'll understand.

BD and I met one October Sunday at church of all places. We had both been attending this small Southern California church for right around three years and had never spoken a word to one another.

Not to say I didn't notice him. His rebellious, musician persona intrigued me far before we exchanged words. At times throughout the three years, I would jokingly declare him as my "church boyfriend" to my close friends. He didn't appear as a cliché, boring churchgoer (my biggest fear). Instead, he had an edge to him and style that didn't repulse me. Even before we met, I sensed we would be a good match.

Yes, you read that correctly, we met at church. The sappiest of all answers when people would ask us how the two of us got together. We would always think of how to make the answer a little more entertaining. We met at church (insert *awwww*). We were both volunteering in a ministry for ex-convicts. No such luck! Just the dull and boring, what every parent dreams of, met-at-church story. Little did I know, our story would end with absolutely nothing pure and boring about it.

After our initial meeting, we spent one full week emailing, G-chatting, texting, calling, and hand-holding. We were smitten! And Facebook official!

Very shortly after that, friends and family were met by all. BD's family drew me in. They were a big faith-based family, who I got along famously with. Immediately, I clicked with all of them, and saw my life as one of them. The vision of our future was strong from the very start. My family also saw BD as their own. His charismatic charm had them hooked. He knew how to work a crowd, and for most of my family and friends, this panned out quite well for him. A few of my friends voiced their reservations about our relationship initially. These reservations included how quickly we began dating, BD's (at times) inappropriate humor, and the stories they knew of his past. However, over time these friends got to know the depth of his personality I fell in love with and were on board.

We jumped right in, infatuation at an all-time high. It appeared as if we had met at the exact right time. BD had just come out of a rebellious phase, now ready to finish his degree and get serious about his faith again. And I was mellowing out of a rather rigid and legalistic phase that was in desperate need of a little refining. We were the balance that made the other better! We dated for two wonderful years of traveling, job promotions, whiskey drinking, romantic dinners, road trips, and all sorts of laughter in between.

All kinds of laughter in between? True! No red flags in sight? False! BD always liked a stiff drink (who doesn't), and a lot of them! I saw this habit as one he would outgrow as he moved forward in his life. For the most part, I would say this was true. He wasn't hittin' the bottle hard every moment of our married life. I viewed this as the natural progression of party when you're young, grow up into a life of responsibility, and leave the wild ways behind.

Now, onto the other, rather daunting flag. BD always had girl "friends" when we were dating. I knew of the friendships he had, but never the extent of them. I recall random text messages he would receive from female co-workers saying, "I miss you," or "Wish you were here." In hindsight, my reaction to these sporadic interactions was on the naive optimist side. I knew he felt that he related better with girls. I would say this had some truth to it, but I never agreed that friendships with the opposite gender were a good idea when you're in a serious relationship. The ironic part is that he also agreed, but never gave up the friendships, making for a merry-go-round conversation that I assumed would resolve itself.

Red flags, blah, blah. Let's go back to the fun for a moment. We had this amazing way of bringing fun to whatever it was we were doing. However, more important than the fun, was that we agreed on all of the "real" stuff. We agreed on our faith, our values, how to foster a healthy marriage, and how we wanted to raise our family. We agreed on everything concerning the foundational components that make up a marriage/family and how to build a good one. Fun and laughter aside, this was the core of why I wanted to marry this man. And marry him I did! A picture-perfect engagement full of blissful planning, intensive pre-marital counseling, and heartfelt love notes promising each other our entire beings. We had a beautiful San Diego church and country club wedding with two hundred of our closest friends and family members.

The first year of marriage the hardest? Maybe. Not sure how much I agree with everyone's hurricane warning. For us, we came into the marriage with very different levels of sexual experience. This led to some frustration and unmet expectations. I would best describe this perfect storm as the Virgin Mary meets the Central Coast Sampler. Our sex life was a communication roadblock for us at times. Since we were so early in our marriage, I assumed that we would have years to work on this, and we both appeared to be more than willing to improve this area of intimacy. Part of learning the dynamic of marriage is sifting through all the brokenness that is brought to the union. We all have a lot of junk from our past, whether it be past romantic relationships or family issues, it will impact how you operate in a marriage.

Back to the flag-waving for a moment. I attributed BD's red flags to immaturity in men before they marry. Some habits and friendships are not meant for marriage. I've seen it before, and I am a firm believer that sometimes the love and stability of a good wife is what a man needs to leave his foolish ways behind. Partnered, of course, with the desire to grow up and move forward in life. The red flags in the marriage were much less. The girl friendships (to my knowledge) were not in the mix. And the drinking rarely struck me as abnormal.

A little before our first year anniversary, I found out I was pregnant! This news came on the exact morning we closed escrow on our house. Whoa, whoa! Major life changes all at once. Watch out! Now just to be clear, our baby was planned (and so was our house, you don't just accidentally sign a million papers in hopes of a thirty-year mortgage), but we did not expect to get pregnant the first month we tried. We had a lot of friends and family members who struggled to get pregnant, so we wanted to have realistic expectations. Even though it was unexpected news at first, the only way you can look at the blessing of a child is just that, a complete blessing. We took the birth classes, revamped our 1970s fixer-upper, and then welcomed our sweet baby girl (after twenty-four hours of drug-free labor)!

Welcoming our daughter into our family unit was such a beautiful time in our marriage. The love we had for each other had created another small human being that we were responsible for loving, raising, teaching, and nurturing. Seeing our love for each other multiply into this crazy love we had for our child was such a surreal experience. There is just nothing like the love you have for your child. Words can't do it justice so I will stop here. A definite upside to our growing family was that we agreed on all of the big parenting decisions: sleep training, schedules, discipline techniques, the division of labor, you name it! It eased us into this next stage of our life together.

For most of our marriage, I have extremely fond memories. BD was always putting me first, affirming everything I did for him, feeling very proud that I was his wife, bragging about me to friends and family, writing me sweet notes around the house, and constantly complimenting me (nine months pregnant and two months postpartum included). I always felt like we were "that couple." We had this too-good-to-be-true, adorable relationship, where we were always laughing. He was never short on affection. Always trying to sneak a make-out sesh in the kitchen, or in public—or in front of his parents, for that matter! We went on fun dates and adventured to new places. He was my personal chef/bartender, and I was his cute little homemaker. We loved having date nights in, complete with fancy dinners and endless wine, or going out to try the latest trendy restaurant. We both felt lucky to have the other. Quite the works in my opinion.

When BD was asked by a co-worker how to describe his spouse, he wrote this:

"Lauren fits me like a puzzle piece. She is the most positive and optimistic person I have ever met. So she makes up for my paranoia and fits of "emo-ness." She is loving and encouraging, emotionally stable, she thinks critically, and always wants to learn. She gives of herself sacrificially, always putting others first, especially me. She lives a perfect definition of love. She has my sense of humor, or what mine would be if I had a filter. We spend most of our time together laughing. And most importantly, we believe the same things. Our philosophies are congruent, and we have the same religious views. We go together perfectly."

2. IT'S ALL OKAY UNTIL IT'S NOT

When you see a drunk girl in a skintight dress at a one-year old's birthday straddling her boyfriend while giving your husband the eye, trust your gut. This bitch is out to wreck your home.

As soon as you enter parenthood, all of a sudden every person with kids the same age as yours is your "friend," meaning you attend a lot of first birthday parties of newfound acquaintances. Put on by proud parents who have thought of every possible detail to make this the perfect first birthday. This particular first birthday, I noticed only one detail, and that was a party guest who appeared to be rather smitten with my husband.

In the fall of 2012 (no pun intended), I noticed a significant change in BD. Our conversations were distant, and I couldn't put my finger on why.

Something about us was out of sync. Our relationship had been pretty off since late September. And by off, I know now, he was living a double life. Dealing with that mental torment is bound to make anyone a little "off." However, in my mind, I thought we were in a little rut, a dry spell, a time where we weren't giddy in love. These times are natural in marriage, and I was convinced this was where it ended.

During what I had defined as a rut, BD would go on "long drives" to "clear his mind." Some nights we would put our daughter to bed, and then he would immediately leave for a drive. His good-byes were never angry or displeased, but distant. If I remember correctly, I imagined the alone time on these "drives" sparking his creativity. Optimism aside, I knew he was struggling with something pretty hard.

Mentally, he resided elsewhere. When I would ask to discuss just what the hell was going on with him (in a much kinder, godlier wife tone of voice), he would put it off and ask for more time to himself. I believe there are times as individuals where you do need to process on a solo level to bring a better version of yourself back to the marriage. I had this scenario in mind when giving BD the benefit of the doubt.

Not to say my mind did not wander and build up what in the world was going on. I remember thinking to myself, *I wonder if he's killed someone? What would I do? Would I stay married to him if he was convicted of murder?* He was acting THAT strange. Clearly, my mind was far from the possibility of an affair. I thought dead body in a field over infidelity. This illustrates just how odd he was acting, and just how much confidence I had in my marriage.

Thinking back to what our family experienced during that season deeply saddens me. Our little family was growing in number and successes. BD had finished his master's program, and we celebrated a promotion at his job. It was our daughter's first Halloween and first birthday. A friend of mine took amazing photos of us to document this time, making for my all-time favorite Christmas cards. The holiday season came, and that meant all of the family traditions that make having a young family so amazing. Knowing that each of these moments we experienced were paired with the other woman on the sidelines is sickening.

A little before Christmas we took off for some "couple time" in Palm Springs. We were firm believers in taking time for our marriage post-baby. Date nights, weekend trips, you name it, we did what needed to be done to keep our marriage strong now that we had a baby. However, this trip was not a pick-me-up rendezvous. BD had an edge to him. The fun we were having had an underlying feeling that something was just not right. One conversation on the trip even led to BD randomly breaking out in tears. His deep anguish became all the more apparent.

On the drive home, when attempting to discuss what the heart of the matter was, he just told me, "It's really bad, and I don't think it can be fixed." Now it was my turn for the tears. That long desert drive I love so dearly suddenly looked like a desolate blur of sand and rocks. We went home to Christmas and New Year's, which all felt like a fraud. Not one of our loved ones sensed anything wrong with our picture-perfect family.

The day after Christmas we had planned to see some friends. These friends were the same ones from the first birthday I referenced earlier. This would be the second time I had any interaction with the home-wrecker. The initial one was with her drunk and straddling, shooting my husband seductive looks. At this point, I sensed an odd vibe between the two of them. He had made mention they had become close friends at work. And by the end of this afternoon hang out, I asked him what exactly they shared with one another. How much did she know about me, our marriage, and our family? He voiced that their friendship was casual. In reality, there was nothing casual going on between them.

Only a couple days into 2013, the confidence I had in my marriage came crashing down. BD and I had planned on finally talking about all of the madness that was going on. The night that this conversation was to take place, BD left to get a pack of cigarettes in preparation for what was to come. I would have asked him to grab me a pack had I known what would transpire during this night. While at the liquor store, I saw that he had left his cell phone. It was on a ledge in the entryway of our home, a common place for us to keep our phones. I still wonder if he left it on purpose as a cowardly way to pave the conversation that was about to happen. The cell phone showed a message, so with no ill intent, I glanced and saw a text message that utterly shocked me. It was a dialogue between him and another friend all about how much he loved the home-wrecker (again, the most respectful label I could come up with for this particular content). The conversation went a little something like, "You just need to tell Lauren … I know I need to tell her … Does the home-wrecker know how much I love her? … She does. And you deserve to be happy. Tell Lauren you're leaving."

BD came home to quite the shit storm. I could not believe what I was reading. The pit in my stomach was as deep as they come. All I could think was somebody better pinch me soon because this must be a horrible, horrible dream. This can't be happening. How did this happen? This type of thing doesn't happen to people like us. What will my family and friends think? The conversation from that evening was one of deep stomach sobbing hows and whys. Here is a journal excerpt from the day after I found out:

"This year will possibly be the hardest one yet. My marriage is in trouble, my heart is broken, and I've been betrayed by the man who I am supposed to share the most intimate parts of my life with. I have hope in the Lord. I have hope that He can redeem, restore, and rebuild. I pray in the name of Jesus that this will be true of our marriage.

Isaiah 40:29
"He gives power to the weak
and strength to the powerless."

Over the course of the following month, I heard three versions of BD's story regarding the affair. The first, second, and third versions. The PG, the R, and the X-rated versions. I don't feel the need to spell out all of the gory details; rehashing is not healthy or helpful. Let's just say an inappropriate friendship including a handful of emails, turned into seeing each other outside of work a couple of times, turned into every worst-case scenario you can think of happening and had been happening for the past four months. I will never forget where we sat in our living room the night he finally confessed to the X-rated version. He acted so nonchalant about his relations with the home-wrecker, and then left for the evening, our daughter sound asleep in her bedroom, me hysterical on the couch.

Once this X-rated version surfaced, I asked BD to move out. I was not going to settle for that level of disrespect in my marriage. I wanted him to take the time to figure out what life he wanted. Conversations that followed in this hellish period included a lot of outlandish comments. Angry eyes accompanied all of these statements. These are the eyes that BD took on when news of the affair came out. They are exactly what they sound like. His eyes were scary, shallow, and all-around angry. What came out of his mouth sounded something like this: "I've never loved you. I married you for the wrong reasons. We have no physical or emotional intimacy. We have no chemistry. I am in love with the home-wrecker, and she owns me."

Here's the thing, I am not going to turn the other cheek to the reasons given (even if they were pretty damn shocking at the time). Did he marry me for the wrong reasons? Possibly. Maybe he thought marrying me was his one saving grace. A redeeming life decision to make up for all of the other poor choices. Sure, that makes some twisted sense. Did we have sex from the movies every night (only two years in)? Not all the time. In my mind, we were still learning the ropes. Did we have intellectually, mind-blowing conversations every night of the week that left us emotionally in sync every day? No, but we both loved learning, sharing, and thinking critically.

All of the reasons given seemed that they could be worked through, had there been a real commitment on his end. I will make this point time and time again, regardless of why you got married (with extreme exceptions), when you are committed to your spouse and have a family together, you can always find a way to thrive as a couple. And I am not talking just bare bones going through the motions of life. If you both want your marriage to work out and improve, it will. Any two committed spouses can make it work.

3. HOME-WRECKERS NEED FATHERS

Much of my initial shock came with the disgusted confusion of what type of girl would do such a thing. This struck a real chord in me. I became very passionate about family structure, and more specifically, a man's role in the family. John Mayer's *Daughters* says it all, "Fathers be good to your daughters, daughters will love like you do." This falls on men, and men alone. Rarely has there ever been a girl to come after a married man (with an infant daughter, in my case) who had a secure relationship with her father and a healthy marriage modeled by her parents.

Men who have daughters must show them love and cherish them so their security won't come from the wrong places. Don't make them wonder how you feel about them or their mommy. Make it known. The obsession should be obnoxious.

James Dobson of *Focus on the Family* stated, "Fathers have an incalculable impact on their daughters. Most psychologists believe, and I am one of them, that all future romantic relationships are influenced positively or negatively by the way a girl interacts with her dad in the childhood years. If that is true, then fathers should give careful thought to this responsibility and seek to be what their daughters need of them."

He goes on to list suggestions for men who have daughters. These two hit home for me:

"I think it is good to begin 'dating' a daughter when she is six years of age, or even earlier. Dad should let the child help plan their evenings, and then see that they occur when and where promised. These times together are not intended simply for fun, although that is important. The father can also use them to show his daughter how a man treats a woman he respects. He can open doors for her, help her with her chair, and listen attentively when she speaks. Later, when she is a teenager, she will know what to expect—or insist on—from the boys she dates."

"A dad should always look for ways to build the self-confidence of his little girl. If she believes he thinks she is pretty and 'special,' she will be inclined to see herself that way. He holds the key to her self-acceptance."

When we found out we were having a daughter, BD and I had many conversations about why so many girls in our society today have such horrible "daddy issues." Having an affair hit so early into our marriage was surprising because of all we had talked about to protect our daughter from ever having to deal with the issues that can come from a broken home. BD and I always agreed that part of being a parent is taking on the role of showing your child how to develop healthy relationships. At our daughter's baptism, the deacon who baptized her said, "The greatest gift you can give your daughter is a loving marriage." I will never forget this gem. Children crave the security of a stable and loving marriage.

A big part of keeping a marriage stable is protecting it. Marriage is susceptible to all sorts of crazy influences. Protecting your marriage, in turn, protects your children and their children. Selfish decisions do not just break up the union between a man and his wife, but the future generations that make up a family unit.

Regardless if you have children, protecting your marriage is crucial in the current state of our world. Always make it a point to protect your marriage against all else. As much as my perspective has a lot to do with men and their role in the family, as to why home-wreckers exist in the first place, it's still a team effort to keep them away.

Take precautions to make sure that each partner is satisfied with the state of the marriage, knowing full well that you are dealing with two imperfect people living in one union. Be mindful of technology and how potentially harmful it can be to your marriage. In the corrupt culture we live in, technology brings a lot more evil than good. It can completely take down your marriage if you let it. I am convinced it did a great deal in destroying mine. And I'm not talking about the obvious porn addiction. I am talking about Facebook messaging and exchanging cell phone numbers with co-workers.

One stand-up blog I frequent is *To Love, Honor, and Vacuum*. I found this goodness that spells out my exact views on technology and how times have a changed.

"It's 1975 and Mr. Company Manager needs to talk to Ms. Sales Manager about an account. It's after hours, so he picks up the phone and calls her at home. Her husband answers. The two chat for a bit about the latest Maple Leafs' loss, and then husband passes the phone to wife.

It's 1991, and Miss Recent Law Grad needs to talk to Mr. Lawyer Partner about a case on the weekend. She dials his home phone and Mr. Lawyer's four-year-old son answers. Recent Law Grad convinces him to pass the phone to his mommy, who explains that Mr. Lawyer Partner is out taking the eight-year-old to gymnastics. Miss Recent Law Grad used to take gymnastics, too. They chat for a bit about the lessons, and she leaves a message with Mrs. Lawyer Partner explaining why she's bugging Mr. Lawyer Partner at home.

It's 1982 and Johnny Doe is driving through his hometown when he passes the old "make-out bridge." He has fleeting thoughts of Mary Jane, with whom he often frequented that spot. But he

25

doesn't look her up because he has no idea where she is. She's probably married anyhow.

Now it's 2013, so let's redo all of those scenarios. Mr. Company Manager texts Ms. Sales Manager about the account. They banter back and forth in texts that grow increasingly personal. He never actually talks to Ms. Sales Manager's husband, and thus often forgets the man exists.

Miss Recent Law Grad texts Mr. Lawyer Partner while he's watching gymnastics. She's never talked to the wife. She knows vaguely that he has a few kids, but they're not real to her. But every day she and the partner text back and forth at least a dozen times. They're becoming good friends.

And Johnny Doe? He found Mary Jane on Facebook a couple of months back. They've been privately messaging for a while now. She's been married for twenty-three years, but she feels dissatisfied. 'Talking' to Johnny reminds her of those exhilarating times when she was young and felt desirable and the future was all open to her. Her husband has no idea that she's found Johnny again."

If technology catches your marriage or spouse at a weak moment and feelings are on the up and up, it's a real recipe for disaster.

On to my next, and probably most adamant point, the importance of keeping your feelings in check. Feelings are deceptive. The heart can lead you to wicked places. "In any relationship, there will be frightening spells in which your feelings of love dry up. And when that happens you must remember that the essence of marriage is that it is a covenant, a commitment, a promise of future love. So what do you do? You do the acts of love, despite your lack of feeling. You may not feel tender, sympathetic, and eager to please, but in your actions, you must BE tender, understanding, forgiving, and helpful. And, if you do that, as time goes on you will not only get through the dry spells, but they will become less frequent and deep, and you will become more constant in your feelings. This is what can happen if you decide to love." – Tim Keller.

Another outstanding blog I came across during the trek to save my marriage was *Nitty Gritty Love*, which just tells everything straight up. My favorite advice is blunt, practical, and realistic (all of which

I hope this book gives to you). This is an excerpt from the post "Follow Your Heart (and other bad ideas)."

"There will be times you feel hopeless. You will even wonder if happiness is possible. You will be tempted to look for greener grass, but as we know, the grass is greener where you water it. Your heart will encourage you to be self-serving, and it will convince you that you need more. I hate to break it to you, but your heart is a filthy liar. My heart has been such a jerk to me; I just can't rely on it anymore. 'The heart is deceitful above all things, and desperately sick, who can understand it?' Jeremiah 17:9 refers to our will, thoughts, motivations, and emotions. Following our hearts sounds nice until others around us want to follow theirs at our expense. If we all focus on simply what makes us feel good, there will be hurting people everywhere."

This excerpt perfectly illustrates just what happens when we are not protecting our hearts from the maddening emotional experiences out there. Protect your marriage from deceptive feelings and the downward spiral of lies they tell you. Hold onto your marriage tight, for dear life. There's no other way to come out in one piece.

4. THE BLAME GAME

Sadly (and believe me, I wish this weren't the case), it is not all the seductive act of an adulteress as to why any of this happened. Why she picked him, and why he embraced her is not always important. The details that come from the whys are rarely helpful in the healing process. She may have "come after" him, but life is about choices. Every. Day. And when we talk about severity, he broke his lifelong vows and abandoned his marriage. She cheated on a silly boyfriend. There's a big difference.

When I first found out about the whirlwind that was my husband's double life, my mind was playing the rerun-on-steroids game. I would rethink every conversation, every phone call, every place he had been, doubting the truth in all of it. And how easy it is to assign every personal flaw or insecurity to a different portion of why this happened in the first place. If your mind has the tendency to play this game, STOP IT. Now! The reasons husbands cheat have very little to do with their wife. There is no perfect spouse, so why focus on any flaws you brought to the marriage? Any mature beings would voice unmet needs, work together to improve them, and, above all, commit to one another regardless of feelings or circumstances. Welcome to marriage!

The reason they give for why an affair happened is never the real reason. There are much deeper emotional issues behind why a man leaves his wife and family. The selfishness is real and raw. The delusion is thick, and the lies are ones they have clung to for far longer than you know. Don't blame yourself. Nothing about who you are excuses your husband's choices.

One of my lifelines and recommended reads to anyone who has experienced this type of betrayal is *Shattered Vows* by Debra Laaser. It's funny how before this happened to me I would have glanced at this self-help book, thinking to myself, *How dramatic! Get a grip, women!* Now, of course, I see the title of this book as nothing but fitting. Shattered is the only way to describe the state of your world when there has been this deep of heartache. This book helped me understand the whys behind affairs. This is not to say there's a real cookie-cutter solution for every marriage, but there was much light shed on the common issues that lead to an affair.

The chapter I will focus on helps answer "How Could This Have Happened? Who to blame? The wife? The husband? The culture?" Well, let's be real, the reason behind this poor of a choice comes from a web of undealt messes.

"Sexual addiction or infidelity of any kind is really about searching for something that is missing in one's life—and probably has been missing for a very long time. It is about using a false substitute for something genuine that is desired. It is an intimacy disorder—a need to connect at a deep emotional and spiritual level with one's spouse and with others but a lack of the skills to do so. The problem, then, is much deeper than sexual impurity itself. It is about a yearning for something more and a determination to find more—even at emotional, spiritual, and relational prices no human being can afford.

"The problem is never the problem! The way we cope with the problem is the problem … Sexual acting out is always a sinful choice. Still, you need to understand that it is about coping with feelings such as anger, fear, loneliness, sadness, anxiety, bored, and disappointment."

"I want you to hear again: your husband's sexual betrayal is not about you. You didn't cause it. It is one of his ways of coping with painful feelings, and it is a horrible, sinful choice. All coping is destructive to those who turn to it. Over time and with repetition, any coping mechanism can become addictive. And whether it is sex or food or work or rage or withdrawal, the consequence of turning toward coping mechanisms instead of safe people and healthy choices is that you will slowly lose your heart—your connection to God and to people you love."

These words were, and on the hard days, still are my saving grace. It is imperative that you do not wear the weight of your husband's poor choices in any way, shape, or form. New insecurities will be coming at you hard, fight 'em off. Hold on to the core of who you are. Remind yourself of your favorite qualities. It may seem silly, and some may even deem it vain, but for the time being, it's very necessary.

Don't focus on why your husband made the choices he did. You can't control his choices. You can't control his desires. And you sure as hell can't navigate the path he will ultimately take. However, you can control your reactions to this horrible hand you've been dealt. You can control what you allow your mind to fixate on. Above all, you can control the path you take, the one lined with hope and healing that will move you forward.

5. WHEN IN LIMBO

"Death itself would be easier to tolerate than being tossed aside like an old shoe. Those who have experienced such a loss tell me that the most painful aspect is their own loneliness— knowing that their unfaithful partner is comforted in the embrace of another."

– James Dobson

During the time we were separated, the emotions I experienced ranged from the lowest pits of heartache to the most hopeful of optimists. Allow yourself both. You ARE going through hell. There's nothing worse. Don't pretend otherwise, but get through each moment, one by one. Moments of joy will come that have nothing to do with the state of your marriage. This is good! Take the happiness when it comes. Do what you can to take care of your soul, and be proactive about keeping yourself in a healthy state of mind. Keep your mind in check, focused on all that is right and just. Wondering what or who your husband is doing will not help anyone. Focus on what will help the healing of your current heart and mind. Don't get too ahead of yourself. It's all a lot to take in.

What helps the empty bed and lonely nights? Well, there are many ways to fill that void. Ones that don't include other men in that empty bed. Stay super busy, make dinner plans, find a new favorite TV show (a comedy), go outside, bask in the sunshine, surround yourself with encouraging people, be honest with yourself about what you need, and communicate those needs to loved ones.

Think about yourself and maintain self-respect, but make the decision to be a fighter. Your husband has been taken from you. Nothing about this was your doing. Will you sit back and play the victim, or will you pull out the big guns and give your marriage the 110 percent you agreed to on your wedding day? Fight with power to keep your marriage and family together. That is the way it was intended to be. Some seasons of marriage are lighthearted, all full of laughter and joy. Others bring us to dark and desperate places. These seasons are only meant for the strong of heart. The ones who won't give up on the vows they spoke.

When you've been hurt in unimaginable ways, it is time to fight with unimaginable might. And this doesn't have to be made known to your husband necessarily. If he's left you, I recommend you sharing very little about where you stand concerning the marriage. It may seem childish, but it is how they operate (like children). Tough love at its finest. James Dobson wrote an excellent book called *Love Must Be Tough*.

Here are a few of my favorite and most helpful excerpts:

"Some especially immature people absolutely have to feel there is a challenge in the relationship to be satisfied with it. Such individuals might even need to hear the door starting to close on the marriage before wanting to hustle back inside.

'Ridiculous!' you say. Of course, it is. We only have one life to live so why spend it testing our loved ones and measuring the limits of their endurance. I don't know. But that's the way we are made. Why else will a toddler or a five-year-old or a teenager deliberately disobey his parents for no other reason than to determine how far Mom and Dad can be pushed? That same urge to test the limits causes students to harass teachers, employees to challenge bosses, privates to disobey sergeants, and so on. And regrettably, it leads some husbands and wives to test the ones they love, too. What is required in each instance is discipline and self-respect by the one on trial."

"Instead of begging, pleading, wringing your hands, and whimpering like an abused puppy, you as the vulnerable partner must appear strangely calm and assured. The key word is confidence, and it is of maximum importance. Your manner should say, 'I believe in me. I'm no longer afraid. I can cope, regardless of the outcome. I know something I'm not talking about. I've had my day of sorrow, and I'm through crying. God and I can handle whatever life puts in the path.'"

"Not that you should say these things with words, of course. In fact, the less said about your frame of mind, the better. It's your private business. One of the great errors made by the vulnerable lover when things begin to deteriorate is to talk too much. The secure partner is non-communicative, evasive, deceptive, and mysterious. He will not sit down and explain his inner feelings to the one who desperately needs that information."

"The partner who is threatening to leave or chase another lover is rarely convinced beyond a shadow of a doubt that he's doing the right thing. He's equipped with a God-given conscience, after all, that is hammering him with guilt. You can be quite certain of that. He may appear resolute and determined, but we must assume that a tug-of-war is going on inside."

Love Must Be Tough was a hard pill to swallow for me as I was shifting out of the role of loving and devoted wife. One day it hit me, though. That phrase, "Have your cake and eat it too." BD was having endless helpings of cake. He had his wife, baby, and house in one hand, and the home-wrecking girlfriend in the other. He was living the cheater's dream. This scenario takes much more strategy than the loving and devoted wife had up her sleeve.

He has left you for her (barf). You've been hurt, deeply wronged. But, as long as there's still hope for your marriage, continue protecting whatever character your husband has left. If your marriage is restored and all works out happily ever after (with a shit ton of work), you won't want to justify to people why you stayed and why you're still married. Not everyone NEEDS to know. Sharing with people who will show the support you need is crucial, but be mindful. You have more grace for your husband than your girlfriends or your parents do. You don't want a million awkward dinners in the future.

Come up with a standard and succinct response for anyone who asks where your spouse is, or how you two are doing. This will keep you from telling unnecessary details to unimportant people. I laughed out loud one night while watching *Sex and the City*. One of the main characters, Charlotte, was recently separated from her husband. She was at a party and when someone asked her about the separation she said, "We're separated—not legally separated, nothing legal, oh God, no!" It gets real awkward real fast, and it's easy to ramble. I am not proud to admit how many conversations I found myself in with people who only wanted a one-word answer as to how I was doing and were given the latest episode of *Jerry Springer*. Practice your responses. It will save you from that conversation at the party when you're ranting to a stranger when they simply ask how you are. "Oh, I'm fine, well, not really fine. My husband and I aren't really 'together' right now. But nothing is final and no, we haven't talked to lawyers!"

Keep your head up, keep fighting, and stay true to all of the beautiful things that make you who you are.

6. JUDGE NOT

"If you judge people, you have no time to love them."

– Mother Theresa

I would say I like myself. There's not a whole lot I would change about who I am. However, the one thing that I could do without is what feels like the constant judgments that float around in my mind. I've always been more judgey than I'd like to admit. Some days it seems that before noon I've already judged your outfit, your boyfriend, your bedding, your parenting, and your choice of Instagram filter. You name it, if I'm not careful, my mind will be on the slippery slope toward judgmental bitch. That being said, I do try to redirect my thoughts and not fixate on the tendencies that leave me judging everything in sight.

My perspective shifted during my time of limbo. I was all of a sudden feeling judgment from total strangers. Yes, I brought my one-year-old daughter to happy hour, and yes, she is crying, and yes, I need this drink more than you and your fake boobs (insert the irony of me making a judgment about her latest enhancement).

I look like death in Target? Puffy eyes and pissed-off scowl? Well, turn your dirty look the other way. My husband just left me, out of nowhere, and for no good reason.

Then, there's the age - old comparison/judgment among mothers. Your kid is speaking in full sentences and writing paragraphs at age one? Awesome. Mine is fed and alive. Considering my current circumstances, I'd call that even.

And last, there was the acquaintance judgment. People who didn't know me and only knew half of our story. I could just read their thoughts. Oh, your husband had an affair? You must never put out, not even own a piece of lingerie, never let him go out with friends, probably suffocate all aspirations he has, and demean the hobbies that make him feel alive. You must try to micromanage and control his every move. No wonder he did this. Do you blame him? Disclaimer: Even if each component I listed above contributed to the crumbling of your marriage, it does not give a reason for the selfish act of an affair.

For me, it was worse because I wasn't the stereotype. Our sex life was plenty healthy. And I love lingerie. BD spent countless nights playing ping-pong with his brother. He is a very talented man, and I encouraged him daily to use that talent in every way he could. Hobbies? Oh, he had 'em! From playing drums to making cheese! I stood by every side of him. The confusion lay all the more thick.

You don't know what people are going through or what their story is. If they look like hell in Trader Joe's, give 'em a smile or look the other way. No need for the concerned look of disgust. I am not going to beat a dead horse. Just be careful of the look you give the lady with a baby in the bar. You don't know what her life looks like behind the scenes.

7. ALL YOU NEED IS LOVE (not)

A reporter asked the couple, "How did you manage to stay together for sixty-five years?" The woman replied, "We were born in a time when if something was broken we would fix it, not throw it away."

I love holidays, probably more than the average female. The flowers, the cards, the gifts, the dinners, the cocktails. I just love celebrating! With this in mind, BD took full of advantage of making his grand take-me-back plea on Mother's Day. And was it ever grand. Had he followed through with anything he said that day, we would be sipping pina coladas on a beach in Mexico right now.

Mother's Day morning we went to our favorite restaurant where we'd celebrated many occasions in the past. It's not a real kid type of place, but we brought our sweetie anyhow, and it made it all the more incredible. I sipped mimosas, our daughter was smiley and adorable, and there was the man I married returning from a five-month "deployment" from our marriage. After we had been sitting and sipping for a little while, BD handed me an envelope. Inside the envelope was a heartfelt card (he always had a way with words) and coupons. After I read each coupon, he then went through each one adding his personal explanation.

My journal entry would give the most accurate description of this day:

"I must document the day that BD planned for me yesterday on Mother's Day. He woke up with our sweetie, let me sleep in, they brought me Starbucks, then took me to brunch. At brunch, I opened a card from him and inside the card were 4 handmade coupons.

The coupons were as follows:
Good for One: Exclusive Companion for Life
BD: I broke up with the home-wrecker.

Good for One: Lifetime Cuddle Privileges
BD: I want to move home.

Good for One: Serious Effort at Communication
(as long as it takes)
BD: I want to go to counseling and learn how to
communicate better, for as long as it takes us.

Good for One: Honeymoon the Sequel
BD: I want to take you on a second honeymoon.

As we both had tears in our eyes looking at one
another, he said, "If it's okay with you, I'd like to
put this back on for good." And pulled his
wedding ring out of his pocket.

It was almost better than when he asked to
marry me. It was real, it was genuine, it was sincere.
It was a rubber-meets-the-road proposal of
commitment.

Sounds like the scene of a romantic comedy,
right? Well, in the months to come there was
nothing romantic or comedic about anything in
our marriage.

I knew this was going to be real hard. I knew
that trust needed to be rebuilt and restored. I knew
there'd be sad days and even more awkward ones.
I knew that we needed joint determination for our

marriage to be salvaged. Most disturbing, in a sense, I knew I was going to have to watch my husband go through a breakup.

The day BD moved all of his belongings back into our home was full of crazed emotions. I left for the day with our daughter and gave him time to sift through and re-organize his life back into ours. I recall this day being difficult for him. We didn't go into details of sorts, but he was leaving behind this disgusting whirlwind of elated experiences that he wasn't quite ready to get rid of. Both of our hearts were sad this day, but for different reasons. That night was a fun and familiar one. We watched a movie together, enjoyed some favorite foods, and drank some beer. We felt like us again. The fun was there. Smiles, laughter, and our natural love for one another. If only we could ride that high out for longer than an evening.

The happy would happen, and then, what felt like immediately, the sad came to match it. The next day, I was reorganizing our closet and dresser. Finding places for his clothing to once again live. As I was unpacking a blue duffle bag, I started noticing shirts I didn't recognize. Ones he had most likely purchased with her. A style that wasn't quite mine or his. As I was looking through this overnight bag that he had probably used at all of their slumber parties, I was met with a small, gray Trojan package. I threw up and stopped the unpacking for the day. After all, too much trauma had happened for us to go back to normal overnight. I did have the hope that normal would come back to stay though.

I have a close friend who went through our exact situation, but one year prior. She was my go-to for months. She warned me of emotions I could have never imagined, and drew out what our first month back together may look like. This particular couple did stay married. They fought for their marriage together. Her husband proved and reproved his trust and devotion. It is only with this mentality on the husband's part that coming back from an affair is possible.

The first month BD was home, he was still in contact with the home-wrecker (behind my back, obviously). Their attachment was strong and seemed to have this delusional power over him. Emotional attachment is a bitch and not easily broken. When the attachment is strong and still alive, no real work can be done on the marriage.

And any work on the marriage that is attempted while said attachment is still alive is not beneficial. It gave BD a false sense of "impossible" because of the fresh twisted heartbreak.

There was a brief stint from the time between when he had lied about still communicating with the other woman and the time he had emotionally checked out where he was making substantial steps toward rebuilding our marriage. He would have his phone readily available for me to see. Any time he went somewhere, he would send me a picture, to comfort and reassure me. He would say things like, "I chose you first, and I am choosing you again. It was always you." These moments were a glimpse into how people actually can work through something this horrific. I felt my trust for him coming back, and our love returning. Again, a high I wish would have lasted for longer than a few weeks.

On top of it all, we had the third party not entirely giving up on her feelings. She once wrote BD an email saying how she missed him and hoped the next time they spoke would be when they were saying their vows. Blah, blah.

BD showed me immediately. We were, after all, working on rebuilding the trust. I felt that it was time to stick up for my marriage. So, instead of ignoring her email, I responded with this:

"After last night's email, I thought it was time for me to contact you. As BD's wife, I'd like to respectfully ask you to please leave him and our family alone. We are working on our marriage, rebuilding what has been broken, and have chosen not to throw away our commitment to one another. This past year has no doubt been a crazy one, full of many lessons for everyone. It has taught me that some years you will need to fight for and defend every last fiber that makes up your marriage. It has also taught me to be on guard for the destruction in the world working against the covenant I made with my husband. Above all, it has motivated me to raise a daughter with enough self-respect that she'd never touch a married man. I hope one day you find a man, who's not already married, to share REAL love and commitment with. We'd all appreciate if you'd leave our marriage alone and let us rebuild what you've tried so hard to destroy."

She never responded, and it wasn't until years later that she contacted me again.

At the two-month mark of BD coming back to our family, he had deemed the marriage impossible. If God wanted to step in and grant a miracle so be it (see Jesus Folk chapter about God intruding upon free will), but that was the only hope for this marriage. During our counseling sessions, BD was often defensive, doubting the program, with all the while no real drive to make this marriage work. Suddenly the coupon about an effort in communication that stated "as long as it takes" had turned into "until the end of the year."

Timeframes are the enemy. Our vows said "as long as we both shall live." Anyone find it odd how there's nothing in a marriage ceremony that states "If things don't get better in six months, I'm filing for divorce?"

This internal decision meant he was done trying to act like a husband because that was not how he felt. He didn't want to treat me like his wife, so he just stopped. As in, would not touch me with a ten-foot pole, was critical about every move I made, and didn't initiate one moment of time together. I was nowhere on his radar. Enduring this rejection did more damage than the affair, the betrayal, the double life, and the lies all put together.

Things get hard in any marriage, especially if you're trying to "save" it, but choices need to be made day in and day out that are working for your partnership. Continually taking blows to your self-esteem never helps anything. I went through months with my husband thoroughly checked out, having no interest in connecting emotionally, physically, socially, or romantically.

At times, I recall glamorizing the love we could have had, had BD been fully committed to staying married. Things would not have been easy. There would have been a lot of rebuilding. A lot of creating connections and passion for one another. A lot of reminding each other we were both in it for keeps. A lot of reassurance to make up for all of the insecurities. A lot of sad and awkward days, grieving the life he left. A lot of self-improvement. A hell of a lot more work than most marriages, no doubt. But why not be your best for the one you committed your life to? I wholeheartedly believe had he committed to a lifelong and unconditional marriage, our story would be full of a unique, joy-filled, and beautiful love created by TWO fighters.

8. THE MAGICAL GARDEN

"Friends are therapists you can drink with."

– Unknown

I would say I was anti-counseling before I went through this traumatic event in my life. I was always so incredibly reasonable that I never understood why people needed a counselor's opinion to guide them through anything. To be clear, this was not an arrogant stance I took, but more so legitimately how I processed things. I felt as if, in my circle of influence, I was the counselor role. It was easy for me to spell out the most reasonable and logical choice in most situations.

When I heard BD's first (PG-rated) version of his story, I called a counseling hotline from an organization I trusted. I felt as if I just needed a little guidance as to what exactly to do when your husband is involved with another woman. This was outside my "reasonable" sphere. When I first called for a free over-the-phone counseling session, I got a recording saying if I left my name and number I'd get a call back in seventy-two hours. The hilarity of this was unreal to me. It felt like I was being put on hold after calling a suicide hotline. Nevertheless, someone called me back the next day and told me something that seemed generic at the time, yet I think of it often. He said, "You can't go outside the marriage to fix the marriage; you must stay in the marriage to fix the marriage." Truth right there. If something about a marriage is not satisfying or meeting an expectation you have, you work with what you have in the marriage; you don't try to satisfy it elsewhere.

During the time we were separated, I went to a counselor who looked like a spitting image of *Mr. Bean*. He was a pretty sensitive guy who drank a lot of green tea (and in turn was frantically running to the bathroom in between clients). When I first started seeing this particular shrink, all I wanted to do was take our daughter from BD and not expose her to any of his filth. I thought maybe this counselor would agree with me, besides I was the victim here. Well, he didn't. He encouraged me to let BD see our daughter for her sake. Our daughter needed to bond with her father. Their relationship needed this time together to thrive. After some convincing on his part, I saw where he was coming from and am thankful for that advice he gave. I never regretted letting our daughter see her father. That was my main take-home from Mr. Bean. All of our other sessions included finding the balance between giving BD time and being a patient wife while protecting myself from the pain and torture his affair was causing. A simple feat (not).

When we started "working" on our marriage, we began a counseling program that was designed to help restore your marriage after an affair. The counselor who developed this program was recommended to us by another couple who'd gone through a similar ordeal. Now, because this man was so well-known for helping couples just like us (in theory), we thought he was completely worth the rate and the drive. The rate was $175 an hour (Anyone else in the wrong profession?). The drive was about an hour and a half from where we were living at the time. Long drives are super fun when you are with someone you enjoy being with. Long drives are super miserable if you were BD and I on our way to "save" our marriage.

On more than one occasion we arrived early to counseling and would head down the street to the local Island's (the only place with a bar in sight) and chug a few beers to ease the nerves. A sweet bartender once asked us why we were laughing and what was the big hurry? Oh us? Just on our way to a marriage counseling program that allegedly saves marriages after an affair. Crickets. Crickets. She responded with sad puppy dog eyes, saying that she was proud of us for wanting to work our marriage.

Now, what struck me as funnier than pre-gaming at Island's was the fact that this counselor was renting an office above a used-car lot. Does it get any more sleazy? How do you take anyone seriously who has an office space at that location? We would walk to the lobby and wait to get buzzed in as another couple was leaving. Every time this shameful transaction took place, each couple staring the other one down, wondering who was the cheater and who was the victim. You'd be surprised. Okay, enough trash-talking about the used-car lot.

This program was full of valuable information if two people were willing and committed. At first, the exercises we did to rebuild trust were very helpful. BD would reassure me till he was blue in the face. He would share with me the type of husband he knew he could be. He would happily talk about our future, and I thought, *I can see how we will rebuild and come back stronger! Wow! This is possible.* Sadly, this didn't last long, and our counseling sessions started to look like this: BD asking what a professional timeframe looked like for improvement in the marriage before calling it quits. BD saying he wasn't attracted to me, didn't want to spend time with me, and had stronger chemistry with the home-wrecker. The counselor all the while looking at me with cancer eyes and telling me how sorry he felt for me. Cancer eyes was a term I created after about the millionth person looked at me with a blank gaze as if I just broke the news that I had terminal cancer. Can I get my money back? Your pity just plummeted what self-esteem I had left.

Before I completely knock this program, I will say there were some beneficial moments. Talking about our pasts in more detail, learning better listening skills/repeating what you hear type activities, diagnosing some personal issues in BD (that he ended up addressing individually), mapping out our marriage highs and lows. One portion that brought an offensively refreshing burst of honesty was when the cheater had to come clean and ask for forgiveness for everything that had ever been done in secret. They would read each point and then ask the question, "Will you forgive me?"

I will never forget looking down at that list as we were about to start the exercise only to see multiple pages. The pages of lies felt as if the word fraud was being stamped across our entire existence. Hearing point after point landed me in one big heartbreaking pit. There were some lies that I doubted forgiveness would ever be possible. However, I understood the potential that this harsh honesty had. I understood the hope for a clean slate was intended for starting fresh with a new, honest marriage.

For people who want to stay married, I'd say that this is beneficial. At the time we did this, I think BD was still on the fence of whether he wanted to stay married (month two). Clearing the air and confessing all secrets the relationship had is the perfect way to start a "new" marriage.

The second portion of the program was dealing with three specific issues that we each had with the marriage. We each voiced these, yet never got to the practical portion of working to improve them. The counselor said he didn't know if he could help us because BD had stated he thought the issues he had were not able to be solved. Who knows if he would have been proved wrong had we completed this program in full, or if I would have just left even more insecure from session after session of cancer eyes and a husband who repeated the words "no attraction, no chemistry, no connection, no desire." This program is a good one for two committed people. Not saying the whole program would be gleeful bliss, but there have been a lot of couples who've had great success in staying married after the completion of this program.

After not completing this program in full due to the hopeless prognosis from the counselor and BD's mind on his way to being made up already, we tried another counselor who specialized in emotional intimacy. This was one area of our marriage BD felt that we lacked. This particular counselor had some good things to say, but his prices were outrageous. Once again, BD was a skeptic about all people or things that would potentially help us. He did inform us that it may take BD years to get over the affair and that I should be open to any new sexual preferences he now had from his time in the affair. It would help him ease the transition back to his marriage. Those words coming from his mouth made me sick to my stomach. We didn't go back to that million-dollar joker.

Which brings us to exploring the idea of an intimacy retreat. They were designed to create emotional and physical intimacy between couples. It was led by a married couple of hippies and took place in the mountains. I thought the idea of this sounded cool and, quite frankly, rather helpful. We talked about it a few times before BD never brought it up again and had no follow-through with committing to anything that could possibly help us. Sound familiar?

After BD had checked out from all counseling endeavors, I started seeking some counseling for myself. In hindsight, this was hilarious. I went to two women. I had only gone to men counselors before because I felt as if I would connect with them better. I had the preconceived notion that female counselors would just be sobbing at the story I told and would only give me emotional advice. I know in reality this was a silly thought and had little truth to it.

Anyhow, I made an appointment with a lady whose office was close by and covered by our insurance. Our first and last meeting went a little something like this... Me telling her our story, her looking at me with a blank stare. Me judging her velvet choker and the fact that she still had price tag stickers on the bottom of her hideous heels, her ranting about how there's no magic number regarding a timeframe for emotional attachment between BD and the home-wrecker. After hearing the phrase, "magic number" another hundred times that hour, I decided to just say no to the velvet choker.

The next and last counselor I went to specialized in sex therapy. Not quite as steamy as it sounds when you're in a celibate marriage. I thought if I somehow could gain something from this type of therapy, then BD would possibly find me more attractive (a horribly depressing thought now that I see it spelled out). For starters, this counselor and I did not have the same views of marriage or sex. You may think that's not the best start. You thought right. She had come from a past of open marriages and communes. She gave me a CD that had different songs to listen to and visualize with to up my pleasure levels. The method consisted of mind-over-matter chants on the road to a garden that would lead you toward "self-satisfaction" and where a man was not needed. Not my cup of tea, or what I hoped to gain from this type of therapy. I wanted to improve my sex life with my husband, not take up chanting in a garden.

Even though this portion of the counseling did not fit in with my realm of thinking, this counselor did do a lot to keep me focused on all of the things in my life that were currently bringing me joy. She encouraged me to keep my days focused on any happiness I could find and not on the husband who looked at me like chopped liver.

Even through all of the crazy moments of counseling, I do now see how it as beneficial. In a marriage, sometimes that third party is necessary (and not how BD would define "third party"). I did learn a lot from the advice of these professionals, and I would encourage women and couples to seek a counselor you connect with and who shares your beliefs. With that being said, I wholeheartedly stand behind that trusted friends who share your beliefs and know you intricately can at times be the best counselors. I suppose, for what it's worth, that's where I stand on counseling. Not quite as anti as I was before, but not completely sold either.

9. FOR THE JESUS FOLK

I hope this chapter doesn't get skipped all too much, as it was the glue that held me together during this hellish season. If you are a Jesus folk going through these hard times, I hope you find comfort in knowing you are not alone in this body of Christ. It's easy to feel as Christians that we are exempt from the awful reality of a broken marriage. Replaying my story, we did everything right in the Christian bubble. We met at and were very involved in our church, dated for a reasonable time, did intensive pre-marital, stayed pure during our dating/engagement, had a happy marriage, and started a sweet family. These components did not add up to a husband's affair. I was very naive to think that my marriage was above something like this.

As alienated as I sometimes felt in the Christian community, God's word had all I needed:

"And I find more bitter than death the woman whose heart is snares and nets, whose hands are fetters. He who pleases God shall escape from her, but the sinner shall be trapped by her." (Ecclesiastes 7:26)

"But the man who commits adultery is an utter fool, for he destroys himself. He will be wounded and disgraced. His shame will never be erased." (Proverbs 6:32–33)

When I read these verses, all I could do was scream, "AMEN!"

During the time BD and I were separated, I prayed nonstop. I prayed 100 percent for the miracle of God restoring our marriage. I would wake up in the middle of the night, and before I even realized I was awake, I was already praying for him. I prayed for conviction in his heart. I prayed that he would desire a righteous life with our little family. I prayed for his man parts to lose function, and for his girlfriend to get fat. I had the faith that God could do anything at any time (which He still can) and that we could have this incredible testimony as a married couple. I was convinced this was going to be the outcome of our story.

I saw firsthand how real the power of prayer was. I felt as if I was in a literal battle for BD's soul. The importance that God puts on marriage and family has Satan attacking it like a serial killer. We had many times where I saw my prayers coming alive in BD and then squashed in the next moment. It seemed that in every step he took toward our marriage, he would be met with a lie pulling him one step away from it.

You may think I'm exaggerating, but there would be days where we would have really great "normal" days together as a couple, feelings were happy and there. Like clockwork, as soon as those days would end, BD would go to sleep and have nightmares of the home-wrecker. He said he felt as if he there was a weight on his chest, and it was suffocating him as he slept. God hears our prayers and honors our obedience, but free will and sin still exist. We must remember how destructive the nature of sin is.

In *The Screwtape Letters*, C. S. Lewis does a phenomenal job at describing just how intricately Satan attacks humans.

"Whatever their bodies do affects their souls. It is funny how mortals always picture us as putting things into their minds: in reality, our best work is done by keeping things out..."

"Nothing is very strong: strong enough to steal away a man's best years not in sweet sins but in a dreary flickering of the mind over it knows not what and knows not why, in the gratification of curiosities so feeble that the man is only half aware of them, in drumming of fingers and kicking of heels, in whistling tunes that he does not like, or in the long, dim labyrinth of reveries that have not even lust or ambition to give them a relish, but which, once chance association has started them, the creature is too weak and fuddled to shake off."

"It does not matter how small the sins are provided that their cumulative effect is to edge the man away from the Light and out into the Nothing. Murder is no better than cards if cards can do the trick. Indeed the safest road to Hell is the gradual one—the gentle slope, soft underfoot, without sudden turnings, without milestones, without signposts."

"Never forget that when we are dealing with any pleasure in its healthy and normal and satisfying form, we are, in a sense, on the Enemy's (God's) ground...He [God] made the pleasure: all our research so far has not enabled us to produce one. All we can do is to encourage the humans to take the pleasures which our Enemy [God] has produced, at times, or in ways, or in degrees, which He [God] has forbidden."

"We must picture hell as a state where everyone is perpetually concerned about his own dignity and advancement, where everyone has a grievance, and where everyone lives with the deadly serious passions of envy, self-importance, and resentment."

Even with all of the ups and downs, the closeness I felt to God during this time was incredible. There I stood, my life barely recognizable. I felt both overwhelmed by the depravity of our world and then at the same time not the slightest bit surprised. Let's be real, as followers of Christ, the Bible is clear that we WILL have trouble, but with that trouble will come a beautiful peace that trumps anything we can wrap our minds around.

John 16:33 says, **"I have told you all this so that you may have peace in me. Here on earth, you will have many trials and sorrows. But take heart, because I have overcome the world."**

I would meditate on this truth: **"And we know God causes everything to work together for the good of those who love God and are called according to his purpose for them."** (Romans 8:28) Why did my "good" look so different from God's? I wanted my life to go back to the good God had for me before this mayhem. It was hard for me to grasp that my "good" and God's good could look so radically different. Was God sparing me from something I couldn't see? Was he protecting me from the wickedness of a rebellious soul?

Well, I found that the answer to all of my questions was this: God wanted me to rest in His peace amongst the chaos. After trying to mend all of the madness myself, I finally surrendered to this gem: **"The Lord will fight for you; you need only be still."** (Exodus 14:14) He wanted me to be still and obedient in the moment. C. S. Lewis put it perfectly, "Never in peace or war, commit your virtue or happiness to the future. Happy work is best done by the man who takes his long-term plans somewhat lightly and works from moment to moment 'as to the Lord.' It is only our daily bread that we are encouraged to ask for. The present is the only time in which any duty can be done or any grace received."

In hindsight, all of the horribly wrong turns turned out to be a level of God's character that had never been present in the rainbows and butterflies. Hour by hour, through all of the sadness and loss, I realized I had never fully experienced this essence of God's comfort. I saw that His comfort was most fully revealed in the absolute pits of sorrow. As time passed, my desired outcome was looking different from God's, but all the while His supernatural comfort was there. The comfort that brought underlying peace, moments of joy, and overall sustenance in a time of downright grief. **"I cried out, 'I am slipping!' but your unfailing love, O Lord, supported me. When doubts**

filled my mind, your comfort gave me renewed hope and cheer." (Psalm 94:18–19)

God's good sometimes looks different than ours, and I learned to trust this truth and look forward to the greater good He had planned. Day by day, God taught me that many of life's richest blessings are the fruit of sorrow or pain. He showed me that some blessings would never be ours unless we are ready to pay the price of pain. After all, redemption, the world's greatest blessing, is the fruit of the world's greatest sorrow. **"God takes our ashes and gives us beauty."** (Isaiah 61:3)

And if you're still fighting for your marriage, be reminded that God is able. The God who walked on water, parted the Red Sea, fed the five thousand, raised Lazarus from the dead, turned water into wine, cleansed the man with leprosy, made the blind man see, and healed the demon-possessed woman can restore and rebuild your marriage! Keep your faith strong, this will give you hope on the real hard days.

I'll end this chapter with all of the Bible verses that kept me afloat:

"The Lord himself will fight for you. Just stay calm." (Exodus 14:14)

"'My thoughts are nothing like your thoughts,' says the Lord. 'And my ways are far beyond anything you could imagine. For just as the heavens are higher than the earth, so my ways are higher than your ways and my thoughts higher than your thoughts.'" (Isaiah 55:8–9)

"I know that you can do anything, and no one can stop you. You asked, 'Who is this that questions my wisdom with such ignorance?' It is I—and I was talking about things I knew nothing about, things far too wonderful for me." (Job 42:1–3)

"The Lord is close to the brokenhearted and saves those who are crushed in spirit." (Psalm 34:18)

"I sought the Lord, and he answered me; he delivered me from all my fears." (Psalm 34:4)

"And my God will meet all your needs according to the riches of his glory in Christ Jesus." (Philippians 4:19)

"May the God of hope fill you with all joy and peace as you trust in Him." (Romans 15:1)

10. THE D WORD

"In every marriage more than a week old, there are grounds for divorce. The trick is to find and continue to find grounds for marriage."

– Robert Anderson

If you and your spouse are still fighting for your marriage, keep at it! I am proud of you. Hold on to the truth that you will be a stronger couple because of it. I have seen many beautiful love stories come from the trials of an affair. If you come out of this, you will have a new level of closeness that only comes from overcoming something this awful. There is a way back from all of this heartache. I have seen it! I was surprised to find out all of the couples who have experienced some infidelity in their marriages. When this happened to me, suddenly those amazing wives you feel like you'd never be even on your best day were telling me about the dark and horrible periods in their marriage. What? In those marriages that look totally perfect and all put together? Yes, in those marriages. Keep going. It will be worth it.

In my case, the choice was made for me. BD left, and a divorce was what he wanted. The year of our divorce, I gave him an anniversary card with one simple word on the front, "Quitter!" Marriages end because one person gave up. Rarely is there a good enough reason other than the selfish lack of gusto. As I said before, I was convinced this was not how our story would end. With that being said, I am not a big fan of denying reality, and mine was the big D.

We took the affordable route and went through mediation. Our mediator was super peppy and always misspelled our names. She grinned her way through our entire first meeting. I just wanted to scream, "Why are you smiling? There's nothing to smile about!" At first, every time I got an email from her my stomach went to knots. Over time, the emails got easier and easier to read (not because there were fewer typos) because emotionally I was healing and detaching.

Being the lover of all things self-help and personal growth, I joined a DivorceCare support group. For me, this particular group was equal parts helpful and depressing. Were there other people in the world going through the same screwed up saga I was? What was wrong with humanity?

It was helpful to commiserate with fellow victims. All of these people were left because of their spouse's poor choices. The part of the group that was tricky for me was the self-evaluation part. What did we all contribute to our marriages that led to this. Well, for me (not to sound conceited), I contributed very little to the end of this marriage. BD would agree with this. On any day of the week. To anyone who asked him. I didn't like that everyone in the group looked at me like I was a crazy person because I had a clear conscience about the fact I didn't contribute to the destruction of my marriage.

This group helped me through a lot of the shame that is tacked on with the D label. "Divorce is not something that defines you, it is something that happened to you." This is a very important point to remember even if you aren't going through a divorce, but simply recovering from an affair. It doesn't define you. It happened to you. It's not who you are. It's something you experienced. Don't allow it too much hold on your future.

DivorceCare taught me a lot about grief. In this shitty time, you're not just processing the loss of a marriage but in actuality a full inventory of losses. You must grieve the loss of your husband, your friend, your lover, your partner, your co-parent, the family you had planned, your next three kids, the bigger house, your travel plans. The list is long, and each one must be grieved.

Divorce is beyond painful. It's painful because:

- You loved your husband with all your heart
- You gave so much of yourself to him
- You worked at the relationship
- You trusted him
- You were faithful
- You thought you'd be together forever

As you may recall, I advised the succinct response for when you're in limbo, well, same goes for when you are going through a divorce. If you are going through a divorce or are already divorced, come up with a standard and succinct response for anyone who asks how you two are doing. It gets easier the more people you tell. The first time I said it out loud, I thought I was going to drop to the fetal position and start sobbing. "We are actually going through a divorce right now… Yes, it is sad, but completely out of my control, so I am doing what I can to move forward." And scene! That covers how you're doing and where you stand on all of it. Boom.

Breaking the news to people varies by the person, their level of friendship, the setting, and how many drinks have been had. Oh, the rants I've given after one too many beers. In all honesty, I felt like I always had to be ready and on guard for a run-in. That family from your old church or your next-door neighbor who moved away or an acquaintance from high school or your hair stylist or the family members you kept in the dark. The list is long, but more often than not, I've found people to be mature and respectful. The majority of people just give you "the best is yet to come" pep talk. Then there was the shock reaction. This always validated and depressed me all at the same time. "Right?! I know! We were a great couple, and I was just as surprised!" and in a different light, "Yes, I know… We were a great couple, and I was completely shocked by it all."

There's nothing easy about divorce, and there's never really a good time to get divorced. You can argue that any stage of life has its pros and cons to completely starting over, but each stage has its own set of heartbreaking moments. For me, I was in my late twenties, and everyone around me was getting married and having more babies. Then there I was, meeting with lawyers, signing divorce papers, and all of a sudden a single mom. Age aside, there's also never a good place to get divorced. At work, for instance. How is one supposed to work with such a heavy heart weighing them down?

For most of my divorce, my job was a stay-at-home mom. It kept me busy, surrounded by my sweet girl and supportive family and mommy friends. However, toward the end, a real job fell in my lap, and I knew financially it was necessary. I not only had to deal with a new stigma of being young and divorced, judged by co-workers, but the divorce wasn't final. I was still receiving emails by the hour from our mediators asking me all sorts of sad and depressing questions. Who will claim our daughter on their taxes, and what will holidays look like? Insert streaming tears as I try to teach long division.

My three main take-homes for getting through the work day are:

- Don't check divorce-related anything (text, emails, phone messages) throughout the day. Wait until your drive home where you can cry in your car, or when you get home and can cry with your glass of wine. This will limit your meltdowns at work.
- Look at work as a mental escape. If there's anything at all you enjoy about your job (which I hope there is), focus on that! Let this be a break from your "real" life. Exercise different parts of your mind that aren't calculating custody schedules or home appraisals.
- Seek out co-workers who are genuine and won't take your story to the rumor mill. This one is huge. Keep your private

life private. People sure do love to talk. You don't need this unnecessary drama. Chances are you have PLENTY of drama without the help of newfound co-workers.

As with all divorce-related obstacles, take it one day at a time and keep a thankful heart. As difficult as going back to work was, I remained grateful for that paycheck and health benefits. You must find those morsels to be thankful for.

"Divorce is the ripping apart of two souls that were meant to be glued together for life. It's never a clean tear, so the mending is not an easy road."

11. SOUL REPAIR

"Time is a revealer and an enabler. If you plant a seed in the ground and water it, in time it will grow and reveal its species. If you plant that same seed and never give it water, it will never grow. In the same way, if you go through the process of healing, in time you will be made whole. But if you skip the healing process, you'll be left wondering why you are the way you are."

– Kris Vallotton

When your world is ripped apart, you are the only one who can repair it. It is hard to sift through the reality that healing has zero to do with the choices of another. There were times where BD would give me these glimmers of hope for our future together and a happily ever after with our sweet family. I had to slap myself, remember all he had done to our marriage, and move toward what I needed to become a healthier version of myself. You are responsible for your healing. This is both your best friend and your worst enemy. It cannot be dependent on the choices of anyone else. Keep reminding yourself of this truth.

Before deciding to act like Mother Theresa and dive into full forgiveness, I beg you not to rush the necessary recovery needed from the pain you've encountered. It will get better, but take every moment as it comes. Experience the pain and move forward. Every single emotion that you feel, and every single loss that you grieve is part of your recovery process. Own it. There's no need in skipping any of it. Fully experiencing it will produce the stronger version of you. And by fully experiencing it, I mean sobbing over a song during your manicure, or going back to a familiar "marriage spot" and making a new memory. The spectrum is long, and every point will help in the healing.

There is much beauty in forgiveness, even if it seems utterly impossible. Keep your mind on that you are forgiving to create the better version of yourself, not because they deserve it. They don't, but who does? When push comes to shove, no one deserves forgiveness.

I spent months where my mind would spin with questions like, *How do you forgive the person who took the life you loved, the heart of your spouse, and the family your daughter deserved?* The act of it was mind-blowing. I knew this was what I eventually needed to accomplish, yet it all seemed so impossible. I read, I prayed, I researched all things forgiveness. I found a helpful book, *The Supernatural Power of Forgiveness* by Kris and Jason Vallotton. This book described a similar betrayal that I had been faced with.

I related with this book on very personal levels. I recall at one point, BD telling me that we simply had no passion for one another. If our life was a card game, I would have screamed from the rooftops, Bullshit! I then read what this book had to offer on "Counterfeit Loves."

"One of love's greatest tragedies is that it's been mistaken for passion. True love is rooted in sacrifice—the laying down and the given of life. Passion is an emotion that is felt most often in the pursuit and exploration of another. We shouldn't exchange passion for love. Nor should the pursuit of passion ever come before the foundation of love."

"Passion is a healthy part of intimate relationships when love is at the core of the covenant. But if a couple uses passion as the glue to bond them together, the relationship will just be a flash fire instead of an eternal flame."

Ah yes. This describes the love between BD and the home-wrecker. It was a counterfeit love. There's something about someone else spelling out exactly what you've experienced to feel less like a crazy person on those bitter days. Reading this and coming to terms with the reality of our situation helped nudge me toward forgiveness.

Supernatural Power of Forgiveness is a great resource for picking up the pieces and moving forward in your marriage, as well. It gives practical ways to rebuild trust. A favorite gem was this, "Trust is not built by the absence of mistakes, but rather on how well we clean up our messes." If you are working to save your marriage, make this your mantra! Your marriage will thank you in twenty years.

DivorceCare also had many grand ideas on forgiveness. It was session eleven of thirteen. They knew it was going to take some easing into. I debated skipping this session many times. They broke it down as follows:

"Forgiveness is the key to healing. Many people don't understand what it means to forgive. It doesn't mean letting your ex off the hook, or saying that what he did was okay. It doesn't mean the same as trust..."

Consequences of Unforgiveness:

- Emotional prison
- Physical effects
- Hurts relationships
- Why we choose bitterness

Forgiveness Is Not:

- Minimizing the hurt or offense
- Trust
- Reconciliation
- Forgetting
- A one-time thing

Forgiveness Is:

- A promise to cancel a debt
- Liberating and healing
- A hard thing to offer
- First a decision, not a feeling. Do not wait until you feel like it.

I made the commitment to forgive BD. I use the word commitment because it's a continual choice. Nothing about it is easy. Nothing about it is deserved. However, the one thing about this particular commitment is that it pieced my heart back together. This choice I make day in and day out is for the greater good. For my daughter, for the other loves in my life, for the better version of myself.

Right around three years post affair, the other woman sent another email (the last one being when BD and I were working on our marriage). Her email offered an apology. Her words illustrated awareness of the destruction she caused. She spoke of her hope for a cordial blended family in the future. She understood if I didn't respond. She understood if I still hated her. In short, my response to her read a little something like this:

"My choice to forgive has been a process that I decided on three years ago, soon after everything went down. I say process because it is a decision I have to make over and over. Some days it's easier than others and some days I am better at it than others. The past is behind us, and life has moved on. People make mistakes, and all we can do at this point is make the most of the situation we are in… I, too, have hopes of a blended family where everyone gets along famously, being that exception to the rule of tension and bitterness. We can navigate through that once it's more of a reality, though. As for now, thank you for reaching out and for showing care for my daughter."

Many advised me not to respond, that she didn't deserve even to hear from me. However, if I've learned anything, it's to keep your peanut gallery safe and protected. I saw her apology as brave and humble. This little back-and-forth between us had me reflecting on the forgiveness that has occurred over the past three years. It always came back to committing to the decision, not the feeling. Ironic how that notion would have kept us from this mess in the first place.

The wisdom of C. S. Lewis acted as an anchor:

"Do not waste time bothering whether you 'love' your neighbor; act as if you did. As soon as we do this we find one of the great secrets. When you are behaving as if you loved someone, you will presently come to love him."

For me, I would replace love with forgiveness in the passage above, although if we are being real, the two go hand in hand. Nothing about forgiveness is easy. Nothing about it is deserved. However, the alternative leaves you in a bitter, emotional prison.

I had the chance to sit down with a dear friend of mine who had spent some time in her life as "the other woman." This role ultimately led to the breakup of her marriage. Her family was devastated, friends were speechless, the general public didn't see it coming. Same old, same old. However, in my conversation with her years after these choices were put to rest, she asked, "How long must people punish me for this?" She had confided in me that her family barely spoke to her, and some friends still wouldn't return her calls. This put an interesting twist on my perception of a home-wrecker. It launched me into my choice to forgive even more so. How long must we punish people for their wrong doings? We end up being more hurt by the choice to hold out on forgiveness. The only alternative to forgiveness is unforgiveness, and as Joyce Meyer puts it, "Unforgiveness is like taking poison and hoping that the other person dies."

12. SQUARE ONE

"There are far, far better things ahead than any we leave behind."

– C. S. Lewis

The label of being divorced frightened me. But the label of being divorced before thirty terrified me. Even though I fought for my marriage and was not at fault, I couldn't possibly explain that to every stranger on the street. I was now the target of so many assumptions I didn't sign up for. I remember driving to my first job interview during the divorce in a total panic. All I could think of were ways to describe to this principal why I was unmarried with a two-year-old daughter. As if my marital status had anything to do with my qualifications as an elementary school teacher.

I would say starting all over was a long and gradual process. It took time, and that's why it was genuine. When BD was in the affair (before I found out), he was acting very odd, and the whole double life was causing a huge disconnect. This started the gradual separation between him and me. When news hit, and he moved out, the general public knew nothing about the troubles in our marriage. We went to weddings together; we celebrated holidays together, and on the surface level, all was as it should be. I was not ready for reality, mostly because I was expecting the huge turnaround on BD's end. I truly acted as if nothing was different. Then when BD came home, I tried desperately for things to go back to our happy-go-lucky, fun-couple selves, but it was just impossible. His attachment to the home-wrecker and lack of desire to be married gave me little to work with. It did help in the continued detachment and healing on my end, though. By the time he moved out the second time, he hadn't hugged me in months, so I didn't miss his affection. He hadn't talked to me all that recently, and the time spent together was nothing quality. Let's just say when he left that second time I wasn't sad because I missed the connection we built, I was just super disappointed that he gave up that easy and left like such a coward.

With all that to say, I did feel like I was unmarried for about a year and a half before the divorce process started. Not because I wanted that status, but because my husband's heart belonged to the home-wrecker.

At this new place in my life, I was not quite ready to jump into a dating relationship. I did make some fun, new friends and would often laugh to myself about what my online dating profile would look like:

Hi! I love Jesus and drinking beer. I have a crazy fun group of girlfriends that are unlike anything I could describe. I don't recycle. Oh! And I'm a mom! I believe in prayer and want my life to look like The Gospel. I also like road trips, picnics, and spontaneity.

Seeking: A man of God who will drink beer with me. A "real" Christian who will love my daughter as much as I do. A critical thinker. A man with mental stability, a non-alcoholic with no history of pill addiction. A real Honest Abe.

Sarcastic and attentive. Affirming, but not smothering. One who welcomes doing things God's way. Oh, and by the way, if we get married, I'll most likely have many specific issues/requests such as NO female friends, mobile phones always in a central location, not really allowed to come home late from work, and your wedding band must be super-glued to your skin... Take a number! Who wants a piece of this?!

I challenged myself to get involved in "young adults" groups that offered social activities, Bible studies, and overall outlets for me to meet other single people. I wasn't looking for my next soul mate, but more just single friends. The majority of my friends were married, and in some of those friendships the dynamic turned to a blurry awkward, something I wasn't all that fond of. Husbands of my friends didn't know how to treat me or what to say. Their cancer eyes were intense, and they were as confused as I was. It was a healthy step for me to switch from couple mode to single mode.

Having our daughter helped a lot more than it hurt, but in terms of moving forward socially, this brought a lot of sadness. I was involved in a moms' group, and for a long time I could not go to any of the organized family events. The idea of being around other young, growing families brought me to tears. Only one year prior we were that adorable family in church, and now I am alone while my daughter spends the day at the beach with BD and the home-wrecker. The brutal reality of this truth did help me to book my days by the hour when I wasn't with my daughter. Instead of surrounding myself with married couples with young children, I would fill my time with all things I enjoy as an individual. It helped ease the pain of the other woman playing house with my daughter.

This new stage was very freeing. Even though it was not the outcome I wanted, it was an outcome. One I could accept, pick up the pieces from, and move forward with. It gave me time to bring back some of the confidence I had lost. It gave me time to become comfortable as a single person, a single mom, a Ms., and the list goes on. I let go of many roles I once loved, and embraced ones I thought I forever let go of at the altar. It was a tough pill to swallow, and there were some real gut-wrenching moments in there. But like everything, as long as you focus on seeing these hard moments as refining your character and transforming you into a stronger person, there's purpose. And there you have it, that's what any hardship is about, finding the stronger you.

13. BANG, BANG

"The world is full of suffering. It is also full of overcoming it."

– Helen Keller

One step forward, two steps back. Damn you, stupid triggers, leave me alone. Triggers of your former life can make the day-to-day just plain difficult. They can take ecstatic joy and turn it into the real ugly kind of crying. They are the reality of letting go of anyone significant in your life. And they come when you least expect it. The best way I found to handle them was to experience the pain they bring and then redirect. Pick up the phone and call a friend who will make you belly laugh. Or text a friend to tell them what a piece of shit your ex is. Or exercise! Get that hot bod you've always wanted. Grab a cocktail with your girlfriends. Take a nice, long walk somewhere beautiful. Do whatever will pick you up. Riding the emotional roller coaster in Triggerland gets exhausting. Take the fast pass on the ride and then run for the emergency exit.

For me, triggers came from just about everywhere. When BD came home, we bought him a white Ranger, the same model of truck that he had when we first met. We were trying to be cute and go back in time. A sweet little plea to start our lives over together and go back to where it all started. At the time, I loved the idea and thought it was adorable. However, when trying to heal and move forward, it was much less adorable. White Rangers were following me. On every highway. In every parking lot. At every stoplight. They were out to get me. Until of course, BD bought the home-wrecker a gray Mazda. It was then that the white Rangers backed off and the gray Mazdas planned their sneaky attack.

I was big into celebrating progress when it came to triggers. The day I could call the home-wrecker by her first name and not a four (or five) letter word, felt like a huge promotion at work, or as if I'd won some contest. I celebrated the progress because I felt like BD threw setbacks my way all the time. He would say they weren't intentional, but he wasn't exactly the most trustworthy guy at the time.

Because of our daughter, we would see each other quite often. This sparked triggers left and right. One night I was on my way back to my home where BD had spent the evening with our daughter. I didn't think to send a courtesy text saying I was on my way home because, well, it was my house I was coming home to, after all. Let's just say I learned that lesson the hard way. I drove up, and he was doing what appeared to be his laundry in my garage. I had talked to him previously about acting a tad too comfortable in my home. This was one specific boundary we had discussed. I don't show up to his bachelor studio to do my laundry, so why should he come to my house to do his. BD agreed to this boundary, and then the second I don't send a text message saying I'm on my way home, the suds are a-spinning. As I drove up, he was shuffling to put all of his dry clothes in his loser college freshman laundry bag when I spotted a pink and red polka dot something. He was doing the home-wrecker's laundry at my house. I couldn't believe my eyes.

Although his track record did consist of doing shocking things to screw with my life, I just thought we were moving past that. I yelled, screamed, and chased him out of my house (not my proudest moment). We didn't discuss it again, and for about a year after the incident I had notes on my washer and dryer saying, *Please do not use.* Signed with a smiley face of sarcasm. With this occurrence, I learned how destructive the retell of a story is.

My reaction to this situation was the most I have ever lost my cool in my entire life. I felt so violated, disgusted, bitter, angry; you name it, I felt it. I screamed every four-letter word in the book, most likely giving my neighbors a show they had never quite seen before. After he had left, I texted my go-to gals telling them what had just happened. The next morning, I woke up with a stomachache and sent out some more recap text messages. And then the retell. I told this story to probably every acquaintance I encountered for the next month. Each time, I brought myself back to the place of emotional turmoil. Yet, I kept at it. Telling and retelling. I needed to vent this one out the day after, no doubt. But not the month after. And the post-it note reminders did not need to stay for an entire year.

Processing life in conversations with friends is so good. It's life-giving. It comforts, encourages, and gives your heart a beautiful hope. However, there's a fine line between sharing with dear friends and the self-inflicted pain from too much retelling. Allow me to share what helped me avoid the over-tell.

Pick Trusted Ears

Be careful who you tell what. There will be times you need someone to just straight agree with you. You need them to tell you that whatever happened really, really sucks. You don't need a solution or a pick-me-up, you just need some affirmation, that yes, the situation does in fact completely blow. Other times, you do want a solution. You want logic when you're all emotion. You want wisdom, prayer, discernment. And then there are the times that you want silence. You want hugs, tears, and quiet. Most likely, you know what friends would fit best in the role that you need. Take some time to think about who you need before you make the initial phone call to spill.

Turn Off the Reruns

As I mentioned earlier, with the laundry incident I told pretty much anyone and everyone who would listen. Sure, it's a killer story. And each new time I told it, I got that same crazed reaction. However, each time I told the story to a new person, their reaction only fueled emotions that I had already processed and dealt with. Check your motives for the retell. Sometimes we do need that extra support. Other times, we repeat our life's stories out of habit, and it regresses our emotional state.

Dwell Elsewhere

If I am not careful, I will dwell and dwell and dwell some more. And I am not talking about the right kind of dwelling, like on an exciting something that just happened. I am talking about the kind of dwelling when you're fixating on something that needs to stay in the past. Letting every detail and word circle your mind. It's all-consuming. Don't allow your mind to rest in moments that have already died. There's never a healthy reason to resurrect those moments.

On to more triggers—during our separation, I was always checking to see if BD was wearing his ring. It turned into this annoyingly compulsive habit that didn't go by the wayside. I would look at married men who wore their rings with stars in my eyes like they could do no harm. Because they wore their wedding ring. Pathetic. Even though BD had taken his ring on and off and then on again and then off when he felt like it and then off for good, I still checked his finger out of habit. I finally got over this annoying tick. It took time, though.

As I said before, I saw BD more often than I would have preferred because of our daughter. This led to casual conversations that leaked information. Little tad bits of information like, oh, that he was living with the other woman. Our divorce process had barely started, and home girl is his new roommate. Bang. Bang.

Then there was the harsh reality that we lived within ten miles of one another, and friends who knew us as that adorable couple. Those same friends would see BD playing a show at a local pub, disgusted to see him with a girl who wasn't me. So many strings attached.

The flip side of the trigger equation deals with all things your ex did perfectly. I nearly had a nervous breakdown (no exaggeration) my first time trying to hang some pictures on the wall. I couldn't get them straight, and then I couldn't spackle correctly. Leaving me with holes in the wall and crooked pictures. For the type A perfectionist that I am, this was a nightmare. BD always hung pictures perfectly straight on the first try. Or there was the Saturday night I attempted to make myself a lemon drop martini and had to throw it down the drain it tasted so foul. How I had messed it up that bad was unreal. In hindsight, I probably should have just chugged it and at least enjoyed the buzz. Having my ex as my personal bartender and chef made my failed culinary attempts all the more painful. Then there was that time when all of the plumbing in the house exploded (I am being dramatic. A pipe broke in my front yard.) Learning or re-learning how to do things on your own is not always an easy task, but it can be done. I have gotten much better at mastering the art of a level, most of my food and drink creations are darn tasty, and I mean, plumbers are great at what they do.

As time goes on, certain triggers once shot through your heart can actually be humorous. Two trigger stories during our divorce come to mind when reflecting upon the progress I had made.

When BD moved out, he took some of our dinner plates. These plates were wedding presents, ones we chose together while we were engaged. I found it odd that he'd want our wedding presents christening his new studio apartment he shared with the home-wrecker. One day he came over and told me he had just bought some new plates, so he wanted to bring ours back. As he started filing them back into my kitchen, I asked, "Who exactly has eaten off of these?" Knowing full well the home-wrecker had dined with them. His face said it all. The next day I took the complete set of Crate & Barrel plates to Goodwill. I imagine they were bought by someone who felt that they had hit the dinnerware jackpot, and now reside in a wonderful kitchen. This experience was a good mark of growth. Had this happened earlier on, those plates would have most likely been Frisbees chucked at BD's head. No Frisbee toss was had, simply a pay-it-forward donation. Deep breath and keep going.

Final Destination: Hell. (Too much?) I always had a great time daydreaming about hilarious happenings I wished upon BD and the other woman. During our divorce, they went on a little vacation together. So romantic, right? I thought about sending a list of prayer requests to all of the local churches. Attention all prayer warriors! My adulterer of a husband is currently on vacation with the woman who took part in destroying my marriage. My prayer requests include: the runs (for one or both of them), bed bugs wherever they lie together, declined credit cards at all bars and restaurants they attend, irritating (but not fatal) car problems. This always brought a smile to my face. The tricky part is you have to know when the hilarity is taking up too much space in your mind. There's a definite balance to the laugh and release! When you can joke about such things (even in a half-kidding fashion), it's sign of progress.

Even with the progress made, some days will just be hard. For me, those days were the special occasions. Holidays bring up every trigger in the book. Only a few short weeks after BD initially left, Hallmark's favorite love holiday greeted me in full force. The timing of this felt like pounds of salt being poured on my broken, wounded heart. As if losing my husband to the other woman wasn't enough, I was now reminded that she would also be his valentine. This very notion still gives me a stomachache if I think about it for long enough. Not spending this day with my husband was a piercing reminder of how much pain I was in. There's nothing worse than a man who's already accounted for in the arms of another, especially on days marked by love and romance.

If you are that broken heart and a special holiday is coming soon, I am sorry. There's nothing worse than feeling like not only is your life in pieces but your heart and soul are as well. Your pain is real and consuming, but here are some tips to get through those triggerful days.

Stay off Social Media

Knowing what all of your friends' boyfriends/fiancés/husbands are doing to make their partner's Valentine's Day or anniversary romantic perfection will not help the state of your heart. Comparison is the thief of joy. When your joy is low, and your heart is hurting, comparison will destroy you.

Keep it Kid-Focused

If you have littles, start the day with heart pancakes and strawberry milk for breakfast. Line up crafts galore. Make love bugs and handmade cards. Break out the heart aprons and bake some festive cookies. Make a special dinner to eat in. Pick a movie, and let your kids stay up late with you. Cuddle up and hold those tiny hands.

Rally Your Single Friends

If you don't have kids, or if you do and would rather go this route... Plan a spa day or day trip with single girlfriends. Have a night in with fun cocktails and a delicious dinner (takeout counts). Line up the romantic comedies, and cheers to the love of good (single) friends.

Treat. Yo. Self.

I must warn you of this slippery slope before I encourage your next big purchase. During the course or my separation and divorce, my home went through a top-to-bottom makeover, new paint, new furniture, new decor. Every holiday (or weekday, at that) warranted a new item. Be careful with this one, but on Valentine's Day, please buy yourself some sort of pick-me-up. It will make for some temporary happiness, which is sometimes the best we can do.

Solo Retreat

It's often difficult to discern the future when you're mid-separation/divorce. There are so many unknowns, and sometimes you really don't know if you're doing the right thing by proceeding with the divorce. Listen, read, and meditate on this day. Spending time alone to spiritually reflect on what to do now, or simply fixating on God's love for you is a peaceful way to get through difficult holidays.

As the years pass, the triggers become less aggressive. Not to say they won't still catch you off guard. One of the most powerful triggers I encountered was after our divorce had been final for almost one full year. This trigger was not an event or a song, it was a plea for reconciliation, bringing to surface our past life as husband and wife. I had imagined this moment in my head many times, and was greeted by a flood of emotions. Validation, anger, hope, confusion, bitterness, justice, pride. This was not the first time he had voiced these regrets.

Initially, his mind was made up, and he had not wanted anything to do with our marriage. As the finality of the divorce was approaching, the comments of regret started. Never were they followed by action, but they happened nonetheless. BD would comment on life with the home-wrecker not being what he had hoped, missing me and the remnants of our little family. And then nothing. Life would go on as if nothing happened. We would interact as if the comments and conversations never took place. These interactions occurred sporadically, but never amounted to much. If I am honest with myself, I would say they held me back emotionally.

When his two-year honeymoon wore off, his conversations with me became more real. His remorse was stronger. Real moments of grief hit him, and I would wonder if our life together would ever work again. What helped combat this emotional trigger was this: You cannot confuse consequences with character. He would come to me when he felt the consequences of his poor choices. This did not change his character. His character was that of someone who did all of this in the first place. Although he expressed sorrow and regret for what had happened, there was no real-life conversion that took place in the meantime. I am a believer that the only way one can truly turn away from their destructive ways is from genuine repentance and a supernatural conversion.

I would remind myself that he is experiencing the natural consequences of the lies he believed in leaving our marriage. I reminded myself that natural consequences to sinful choices are sad. This sadness cannot be confused with repentance and a change in character, though. The fact of the matter is it's sad when a man leaves his family. It's sad when parents have to split time with their child. And it's sad when people live in deep regret for the horrible things they've done. It's all sad.

This sadness does not mean that it's not bringing the greater good to life, though. Heartbreaking circumstances can prepare you for the intricacies of a rich and full life. Sadness cannot be confused with the consistency of one's character. Character is character no matter where you see it. It will carry over. Don't ignore where it dwindles, or exaggerate where it just so happens to do the right thing. Its authenticity will reveal itself over time.

A bit of a rant on that particular triggerful instance, but worth the point I am driving home. Deal with the pain of each trigger as it comes, but take heart in knowing that the pain will soon dwindle away to a distant memory.

14. IF YOU HAVE LITTLES

Do we agree on anything anymore? Religious beliefs? Nope. Moral life decisions? Definitely not. Basic conversation topics? Can't even do that. I remember times where having a simple conversation (post-affair) felt like pulling teeth with a stranger. There was nothing. Our unity was destroyed.

Then there was our daughter, who we'd both take a bullet for. This little being we created with the sweetest smile and the most darling personality. If you're still fighting, trying to live through the long months of a dying marriage: focus on your little one. Remember that this small human being you created represents the love you once had for each other and the love you share for your child. Remember when you decided to have this child, it was in the fine print that your family would stay together forever. Keep your eye on that fine print and fight for your family.

Here's the deal straight up: Kids can't be the reason that two people stay married. The couple needs the desire to keep their marriage a separate, thriving relationship, one that their children see as secure and loving, not based on a child. It's far too much pressure for children to feel that they are what's keeping their family together. It screams emotional immaturity. Kids are a huge motivator to make things work, but you need more.

At times, our daughter was my only motivator, and had there been a shared effort, she would have been a huge driving force. Let's be real, no one wants to share their child with a stepparent. I would've done anything to avoid that.

As much as having a child from a broken marriage adds a level of raw difficulty, it also reminds you there was a purpose for your union. I remind myself daily: I'd go through it all again if it meant I had my daughter.

While talking pure difficulty, your child also holds you to a completely new level of accountability in how you treat and respond to your ex-spouse. DivorceCare had some very helpful "easier said than done" reminders on the topic of co-parenting. This session was titled, "KidCare: Effects of divorce on children. Mistakes parents make and how to avoid them." It started with a downer video clip about how pretty much all children of divorced parents are doomed as human beings and susceptible to drug use, suicide, poor grades, teen pregnancy, depression, and every other worst-case scenario a parent can imagine. Where's the encouragement? This wasn't my daughter's fault. Then it got into how to prevent the terror described in the opening scene. Thank God.

Much like anything that children encounter in their upbringing, how the matter is handled by the parent drastically changes the long-term effects that are had. Our children learn more by observing than any other way, so we must be careful how we handle our anger, conflict, and how we speak of our ex.

Here are the mistakes that parents make (according to DivorceCare):

- Lack of stability
- Lower expectations
- Trashing child's parent
- Keeping child from parent
- Using child to spy on ex
- Putting child in the middle
- Making child choose
- Treating child as an adult
- Dumping child on counselor
- Overindulging children

As a parent whose child will have divorced parents, I'd like to avoid all of the above. I'd say it's a good idea to avoid all of the above as a parent, even if you're married and simply in a rough patch. For me, I take basic parenting principles and apply them to the situation I will forever (I say forever, because we will always be co-parents) be in with BD. The type of parent I attempt to be is one who models unconditional love, forgiveness, self-respect, humility, and kindness regardless of circumstances. I try to show my daughter these qualities in every situation I am faced with.

Obviously, I am human and far from perfect, but I do my best.

I would say that all of these qualities are lumped into the most difficult discipline for me personally, and that would be holding my tongue. He didn't unconditionally love me; I can forgive but not forget. I have self-respect, and that's why he left, my pride often drowns out my humility, and what kind words are to be said about a cheating husband. Rant done. I say discipline because that's exactly what it is. Implementing the no trash talking is a discipline that takes practice. It is not natural nor does it come easy. However, I love my daughter more. My love for her took over my need to be a petty shit talker about her father. Bashing your spouse or ex-spouse is a horrible act any way you look at it.

Remember your child knows that he/she is made up of both of you. If you are talking so negatively about half of them, they will start doubting their worth and self-esteem. If nothing else, remind yourself that your little one would not be here if it weren't for that other parent. The child you adore is half of them and would not exist without them. And repeat.

Then there are those darn holidays again. They take on a new light when divorce hits a family. Scheduling by the hour and anticipated awkwardness filters through what should be a joy-filled celebration. Grief has been huge on my list of all things that make up the holiday season. It was another loss I was grieving from my marriage. The loss of a child waking up with both their parents on Christmas morning to open presents. The loss of our family traditions. The reality of being at Christmas gatherings without my daughter, or her being at them without me. Don't downplay those losses. They are very heartbreaking and must be properly mourned.

My top tips for navigating co-parenting during the holidays are as follows:

Swallow Your Pride

Prepare your heart in prayer for the interactions you'll have. Pray for your parenting example to be one of unconditional love, forgiveness, self-respect, humility, and kindness, regardless of the circumstances.

Focus On Your Child

There's nothing more magical than a child on a holiday. Nothing should squash that excitement. Let their pure bliss take over your situation. Encourage the joy and stay in that place with them.

Check the Trash Talk

As I mentioned earlier, venting is important, but not meant for holiday gatherings. It is meant for the ears of close friends where children are not present. Whatever the occasion may be, give your child the gift of holding your tongue.

The swings of co-parents are still jarring from time to time. Some days you feel like a rock star. Ruling at every part of this crazy life. Laughter comes back, co-parenting is blissful, feeling enamored by your child, and the future seems like it will all be better than just okay. You feel like you've beaten some ridiculous odds, and you'll be that incredible exception to the blended family stereotype. I wish all days were like these ones. For me, there are more of these than the other days.

However, the "other days" feel like the news of your family breaking up just hit you for the first time. Where the thought of your child having two homes feels suffocating. Days when dropping your child off to their other parent feels you are giving up your baby for good. Catching a glance of your child's room, empty in your home, feels as if there's been a death. Why is there no laughter or tantrums or pretend play coming from that room? Why is it silent and stale?

And my two cents on what helps this maddening pendulum? Bask, and I mean saturate, in the good. When you have those moments of your new reality that feel joyful, cling to that emotion and store it. You'll need the reminder on the impossible days.

The last point I'll make about co-parenting your little one took me a long time to wrap my mind around. A shitty husband does not always equal a shitty father. There's no denying BD was far from husband of the year, but as a father, there's much to be thankful for. I know this concept is hard to fathom, especially in the early days of divorce, but it's the truth. Sure, if your ex-husband left the marriage they'll forever have that one major life choice that altered their child's future forever. However, when you're moving forward in that future, your role of the other co-parent (the ex-wife) should not be one of punishment forever because they left the marriage.

This took me TOO LONG to learn and I still have days where all I want to do is punish the heck outta BD for what he did to my daughter's future. However, all I can really ask of BD is that he's a good father to our daughter. My daughter adores him and for good reason. He helps us financially and in the way we split our time. He disciplines our daughter the way we agreed upon. He teaches her and he doesn't spoil her. He shows her love and care. My point is this, it's okay to think your ex is a good father. It's actually more than okay. You can't stay in the punishing judgment stage forever. If you can find things about your fellow co-parent in a positive light, your child will greatly benefit.

Children need their fathers (and mothers) regardless of faults and imperfections, and regardless of what happened in your marriage. Why? Because the minute they came into this world, they earned the right to have the love and nurturing that can only come from parents.

I know you've found yourself in a crazy life that you can't control and didn't sign up for, but what you do have control over working at creating the life you intended for your littles. They are always worth the heartache you've experienced. And they will always be the brightest of all silver lining on those dark days.

15. LIFE GOES ON

"For a seed to achieve its greatest expression, it must come completely undone. The shell cracks, its insides come out and everything changes. To someone who doesn't understand growth, it would look like complete destruction."

– Cynthia Occelli

I adore that Cynthia Occelli describes growth as complete destruction. People who haven't experienced core-shattering growth wouldn't quite understand this illustration, but for me, it spoke to every part of my being. Complete destruction happened. It happened to my marriage, my family, my future, my trust, my mind, my judgment, you name it… Destruction happened. With all growth (destruction), the rebuilding is an articulate, careful, and beautiful process. The rebuilding trumps the damage. This is true for any situation. I don't wish hardship upon anyone, but the growth that comes from it is so unique that in some twisted way, I think humanity should endure it. Maybe we'd all be a tad less self-obsessed? Okay, another day, another book.

Life post-affair can take one of two turns. Your marriage can be saved and restored tenfold. Your family could continue to grow, and you could live the life the two of you had planned, looking at this as a minor (some days major) hiccup. Your story could be the picture of encouragement and hope to all couples who've encountered such trouble. You and your spouse can be stronger than ever with a bond only created by hardship. I pray this is the turn your marriage took. My heart hopes that your marriage is saved, and you can write to me telling me your beaming success story of redemption.

Or one of you will give up, and your marriage won't survive. You will start a whole new life apart from the old.

For me, one of the hardest parts about picking up and starting over is leaving behind the old version of you. Of course, you are still the same individual you were, just with a newfound badass strength, but there are things and roles about yourself you must abandon. I say abandon because it portrays the harshness that needs to happen. Attempting to play the old with the new is always trouble.

Starting my life over was refreshing, but surely had moments of grief. I knew 110 percent that I had given my marriage every fiber of my heart and soul, making moving forward in life number two a peaceful experience. Over time the hard moments got less. Remember to let yourself experience the sad moments for what they are worth, though. A divorce is a sad and devastating process, even if you're handling it like a champ. Call it for what it is. Allow yourself those sad times, because a beautiful time will come where the joyful moments are more than the sad ones. It's bliss, and it happens.

If you are not ready to read about a life number two yet, then put this book away and pick it up when that route doesn't bring you sadness. It took me awhile to stomach starting life all over. I want to share the beautiful hope of a rich life post-divorce, but if you're not ready, and you're still grieving, that must take priority. Fully mourning life number one in all of its losses must happen before moving forward.

For those who are in the place to read about the joy possible for life number two, read on. Life number two meant a second chance that I didn't always want. It meant full circle in a way I didn't anticipate. It meant reinvention. Reinvention spanned from new digs to finding love once again to drinks with the other woman.

New Digs

I redecorated my house when BD moved out the first time, then he moved back in, completely vetoing all purchases meant to start anew. The only solution to this was home makeover take two. This time was more permanent. I knew this space was solely mine, and I could make of it whatever I wanted, much of how I felt about my new life. A couple of years later when all of life was pulling me in a different direction from the location of my home, I did sell the home. I wrote a piece about this experience and the emotions that went on:

Well, I've decided to put my house on the market. This is a decision I have battled with for some time now. My attachment to this home runs deep. I would say it's the final part of my former life that I have yet to let go of. When doors continue to open in one place, and your home is in the other, you must adult up and decide what's best. For me, what's best is leaving this home and starting fresh somewhere new. My new life has been in the works for a while now, and it's time that my home catches up. Thinking about my house for sale brings out every emotion in the book. From real tears streaming down my neck as I sat in my favorite backyard spot, to gleeful excitement as I walked into an open house only a few days later. The swings are real, my friends.

In reflecting on my emotional highs and lows, I started thinking of all the walls of this home have seen... The very first morning waking up in this home, the bathroom walls saw a positive pregnancy test. Every weekend that followed for the next nine months, those walls saw giddy homeowners bonding with friends and family members over house projects, beer (not for the preggo), and pizza. Those walls saw a 1970s fixer-upper made over from top to bottom. They saw newlyweds celebrate their first (and second) wedding anniversary. They saw a crazy pregnant lady pick the wrong exterior paint colors. Those walls welcomed a beautiful baby girl home. They saw parents experience the love of their child, an unreal love like nothing else in this world. Those walls saw a baby's first coos, signs, smiles, laughs, bites, scoots, crawls, words, and steps. They saw baptism parties, thirtieth birthday parties, garage dance parties, graduation parties, baby showers, and first birthday parties. They saw playdates where new mommy friends would sob and vent and laugh about the stay-at-home mom gig not being as easy as they all once thought. They saw family dinners, date nights in, and young married couples gathered, talking about how life has changed in the best possible ways.

And then quite suddenly, these walls saw temptation. They saw a good man taken over by darkness. They saw a husband and father lie to his wife and daughter. They saw a man who was already accounted for getting sucked into to the flattery of an adulteress. They saw early mornings and late nights of deception. They saw details of an affair revealed in a text message. They saw screaming matches and sobbing stomachaches.

They heard more and more lies until they had all been exposed. They saw a wife left alone. They saw a half-empty bed, closet, and dresser. They saw a stay-at-home mom turned single mom. They saw long days with a one-year-old with no daddy relief at the five o'clock hour. They saw girls nights of long hugs, tears, venting, silence, and a whole lot of wine. They heard check-ins by the hour via text messages and phone calls from family members, neighbors, and friends. They saw a desperate, heart-exposed woman. They heard kneeling prayers, begging and pleading with God.

They then saw what appeared to be the start of restoration. They saw a man apprehensively come back to his family and home. They saw him try, but not hard enough. They saw awkward months of a destroyed husband and wife trying to salvage what was left. They saw crying conversations of whys and hows. They heard "How could you's" and "Why did you's" and "I don't get it's." They saw twelve packs finished as discussions, and recaps of counseling sessions took place. They saw brief moments of normalcy in backyard BBQs, kiddie pools, and family time. Only to be followed by long days of setbacks. They saw a downward spiral leading to the decision made to legally end a marriage once and for all. They saw depressing holidays, knowing it was the last all together under one roof. They saw a man leave for the second and final time.

They saw the aftermath of initial meetings with lawyers. They saw tears as a home was split apart in dollar signs. They heard custody discussions of spreading thin the weekdays, weekends, and holidays. They saw some more tears over the thought of a sweet child in two homes. They saw regret and second thoughts and "Are you sure?" and "Is this happening?" They saw a few more screaming matches partnered with this time more bitterness than sadness. They saw the death of a marriage, of a family, and of a life together. They saw loss and grieving.

They saw attempts at reinventing a home and life. They saw Goodwill purges of dishes, wedding presents, and all reminders of a marriage on its way out. They saw new paint colors, furniture, and bedding. They saw remodeled bathrooms and fresh photos on the walls. They saw the process of recovery, healing, and acceptance. They saw a mom, not ready to go back to work, do so anyhow to provide for her baby. They saw shots of straight whiskey as the signing of divorce papers happened, both parties unsure how it got to this point. They saw the look of a final stamp when legal papers were received in the mail. Months later, they heard the conversation of a man who wanted back the life he left. They saw confused emotions in response to his plea. They saw discernment and prayer and more conversations confirming the decision to move forward with separate lives.

They saw a new life start, one grounded in God's faithful goodness. They saw cheer and happiness re-enter the home in a different form. They saw the birth of new dynamics. They saw a focus shifting from the love of a husband and wife to the shared love of their child. They heard co-parenting conversations, and how to blend two new lives into one. They saw a united front of two parents wanting the best for their daughter. They heard laughter over toddler talk, and frustration over toddler tantrums. They saw the potential for a healthy blended family.

Those walls saw a sweet second date of sparks and butterflies. They saw the start of a new love. They saw God's promises revealed. They saw blissful excitement for the future. They saw a family redefined. They saw new bonds form over quality time with Legos, puzzles, and Play-Doh. They heard dreams of starting a new life in a new home. They saw the freedom of leaving the past in the past. They heard conversations of passing on this home to house a new family's memories. They saw tears of sadness and joy, missing a first home and welcoming a second one.

In looking back, I suppose the emotional swings of selling this home make a little more sense now. In five years, these walls have seen and heard more than most experience in a lifetime. And now, as I wait for the right family to buy this house, I'll say, here's to the stories my future walls will tell!

This depicts exactly the emotional happenings that led me to the final decision to sell my home. Don't make sudden moves with life number two. Slow and steady, let your heart, soul, and walls heal.

The Greater Love

My heart begs yours to have no impulsivity in this next part of life number two. My separation/divorce start to finish took two and a half years. During this time, I did not go on one date, nor did I give one man my phone number, nor did I even invest in friendships with guys. I was not ready, and in my mind, it was not appropriate to dabble with another man while I wasn't even officially divorced yet. This was my saving grace. I am in a healthy relationship now because of that time I took to myself. If I could leave you with one morsel of advice, it would be to take time to heal the ugliness of divorce before seeking out love once again.

A few months after my divorce was final, I went out for the night with BD's parents. This was not a rare occurrence. I stayed very close with them and spent a great deal of time with them during the divorce. Earlier that year they had met a man at a country bar they frequent. A conversation was struck up, and they told him that he sure would like their daughter-in-law. Wait, what!? No information was exchanged, just one of those *Hope to see you agains!* That night out, months later at the same country bar, they did see him again, and there I was. And in one night, my life was forever changed. I met my cowboy, my forever love, the man I will spend all of life number two with.

Pump the brakes a bit for a moment. There was a healthy relationship fostered between the night we met and now forever. Dating after an affair/divorce and with a toddler is a much more delicate process than just the single gal's dating strategy. Here are the five pointers of what guided my choices in dating post-divorce. I call it the five-step. (See what I did there? We met at a country bar.)

1. Make Sure Your Marriage is 100-Percent Over

Discern if there is ANY chance at all for reconciliation. If you are still working on your marriage, perhaps in a counseling program, or have a lingering desire (on either end) to stay married, stick to plan A. Dating or letting your heart wander while there is still hope for your marriage will do nothing but add more layers to recover from. Chances are, you'll have enough craziness to deal with, why add yet another party to the mix? Remember, it's not over until it's over.

2. Take Some Time

DivorceCare says a simple equation for when you're ready to date is taking the time you were married and divide it by two. This number is the amount of time it supposedly takes for you to heal emotionally before entering a new relationship. My ex-husband and I were legally married for five years, but he was 100-percent out by year four. Meaning, two years is my magic dating number. It was closer to a year and a half from the time my ex left that I started dating my cowboy. However, it was two and a half years total from the day he left the first time. (So much leaving, who can keep track?)

As you know, I spent this time seeking council, reading, crying, mourning, praying, and authentically healing. How you spend this time will determine how you operate in your future relationships. I am currently in a healthy relationship (with an amazing man) because I spent this time single and grieving.

3. Resist the Rebound

Set the bar as high as they come. Not in an unrealistic, shallow sense, but in a cautious one. Your heart has been through enough, don't inflict any more unnecessary pain. From the start of my separation to the very day my divorce was final, all sorts of random friends were coming at me saying they had someone for me to meet. Any time I would make mention that I was going through a divorce or freshly single, their lightbulb would go off, and all of a sudden everyone was convinced they knew my next soul mate. All of these suitors were slightly off in one way or another. Perhaps there was no attraction, or we didn't share a similar faith, or they weren't all that thrilled that I had a child or (you fill in the blank).

With the online dating world booming, it is so easy to get your profile up, sit back, and wait to see who wants to date you! However, online dating as a divorced person feels less appealing. You can't explain in the 160-character About Me section why exactly you're divorced. I didn't dabble in this enough to give an accurate review, but those are my thoughts nonetheless. It seems that it would be discouraging because you have to check the divorce box, and you can't always explain the whys initially.

After you've experienced the rejection of infidelity and divorce, of course, the attention is nice. However, don't use attention from Joe Schmo to help boost your ego and jolt you into a new relationship. It's always, ALWAYS better to be alone than settling for someone who you're not all that thrilled about.

4. It Will Feel Different (and that's okay)

Oh, the feelings! All the feelings! Falling in love after you've gone through a divorce feels different. Your heart will experience emotions more cautiously, which is natural. It took me awhile to believe that history wouldn't repeat itself. I didn't come from a marriage where we fought or had marital "issues," so BD's affair and all that transpired because of it was shocking. If this could happen to our marriage, it could happen to anyone's—or my next one! It's a process that requires a lot of time and prayer. I will say that the love and reassurance that comes from a quality man helps combat the lie that your second marriage is doomed because of your first.

Ask yourself if you're feeling different simply because of the life stage you are in. Take into account the age you were when your former marriage started versus now. Not only will you feel more guarded because of what you've been through, but by nature falling in love at twenty-two feels different than falling in love at thirty. That's eight years of growth and evolving to take into account. This is far from a bad thing.

Lastly on this one, don't believe the lie that you won't find love again. I do remember feeling like I would NEVER find anyone I would ever love as much, find as funny, or enjoy life with as much. All of which are FALSE. Other lies my mind would tell were that I would NEVER find someone who would want to date a divorced thirty-year-old with possible trust issues, a spunky little three-year-old, and a baby daddy still in the picture. Talk about a handful o' baggage (and lies). Life is unpredictable, and you are who you are because of those unpredictable turn of events. Don't deem that stronger version of yourself who overcame a shit ton of obstacles a bad thing. Most men find strength in a woman to be an attractive quality. You will find love again, and it will be refreshing.

5. Careful with the Kiddos

Before I started dating, I was convinced that I was not going to introduce my daughter to my boyfriend until we were close to getting engaged. I did not want her to witness another man leaving her mommy. Honestly, she's so young, it's doubtful she'd arrive at that conclusion anyhow, but I wanted to be OVERLY cautious.

At the start of my new relationship, I obviously told my man I had a daughter, but I did my best to never put any pressure on the dynamic between the two of them. I wanted to give my relationship enough time to develop on its own before even thinking about adding in the element of my child. And my boyfriend appreciated that I wasn't trying to force him into fatherhood on the second date.

After three months of dating, the two of them met. When they did meet, it was very casual. We treated it like any time my daughter meets a friend of mine. My boyfriend and I didn't show much affection in front of her, and in her mind, he was just another friend. As time went on, we spent more time together, and their relationship developed naturally. *Naturally* is the key word here.

We would go out to lunch, do puzzles, play with Legos, watch movies, go to the park... pretty much activities that take place in my daughter's normal toddler life.

Don't bring a "Disneyland Dad" into your child's life. When the three of us spend time together, it is never extravagant or extreme. He doesn't bring her new toys every time he sees her. He doesn't let her get away with murder and do whatever she wants. He supports and reinforces the way I parent. Their natural bond developed nicely because it was not based on presents or theme parks, but genuine care and quality time.

Finally, NEVER allude that this person is taking the place of your baby daddy (unless your ex is completely out of the picture for legal reasons). Your new love interest is not meant to replace a parent but join the team. We use the term "bonus daddy," which I love. "Step" has such a negative connotation, where bonus just sounds like an added blessing.

My plea for all the single ladies out there is that you would be cautious and patient. The right man who helps undo all of the madness you've experienced is absolutely worth the wait. My cowboy and I are currently engaged, getting married early next year.

Cheers to the Future

Well, if BD's parents introducing to me my future husband isn't enough of a fun twist for you, get ready for this one. BD and the home-wrecker are also planning on getting hitched. Deep breath, I know. When this decision was more or less made, I decided it was time for the other woman (I don't call her that anymore) and I to have a little sit-down. We hadn't seen each other or interacted this entire time. The last time I had seen her was before news of the affair had hit. When she was simply BD's co-worker. I sent her a text message initiating going out for drinks, in which she responded asking if I was sending the message to the right person. Breaking the ice quite nicely. We made plans to meet.

It's funny how time can heal and change your perspective. I remember times mid-affair where I envisioned what would go down had I run into her in public, and let me tell you, it wasn't pretty. There's a reason why this encounter took three years to happen. When we met (again), all I had imagined of her disappeared. I saw her as a human, and not a home-wrecker. All I could have hoped for this sit-down. We shot the shit for a bit, and then got right to it.

My desire to clear the air with her came from wanting my daughter's family unit to be one of peace and not tension. I wanted all parents on the same team. I wanted to hear from her very mouth responses to the tough questions. I didn't want BD sugarcoating a damn thing. And so the questions happened. What will you tell my daughter? I need her to know how wrong this was. And then came the apologies and ownership of how awful everything was. What is your view of marriage? You will be modeling one to my daughter. And then came her answer of permanence and love. We will be raising a daughter together. I want that daughter to have self-respect and never touch a married man. And then came the agreeance of how she will never teach her that this was a good idea or anything she should ever do. I thanked her for her care for my daughter. I thanked her for supporting the parenting model BD and I had put in place. I thanked her for being a team player to raise this little girl the best way we can.

And, just like that, I saw her like anyone else who made a choice they weren't all that proud of. I asked her about her family, her upbringing, her friendships, and simply about who she was. I wanted to get to know her beyond the role as the other woman. This interaction needed to happen in order for my daughter to have a healthy blended family. It brought me to new levels of gratitude for who this woman was in my daughter's life. After all, she could have resented my sweet daughter and not treated her as her own. That would be the worst, much worse than the reality that the other woman will be my daughter's bonus mommy.

We must keep our one shared child the center and motivation for all we do and how we interact. She deserves a peaceable and united family unit regardless of all that went down in the past. She is the innocent victim in all of this, but this does not mean she must suffer through undealt bitterness among the people she loves the most.

There you have it, the hope that is my story. Here I stand, stronger (and happier) than ever, living a life I in no way planned. If the details of your ending are still panning out, take heart. You will heal and be whole once again. As time passes, people won't always remember the details of the saga, but they will remember how you handled yourself while it was going on, and how well you picked up the pieces.

Who you are today is because of what you have experienced in the past. There are certain qualities in a person's character that only come from surviving a traumatic experience. These qualities cannot be created, they can't be worked on, they are not a discipline or skill, they simply belong to those who have overcome. They are our consolation prizes, exceptional and beautiful. Means for celebration.

Celebrate the strength you've received through this hard time in your life. Celebrate the story, all your own. Celebrate the ending you created and embraced. And above all, dear ones, celebrate that you are in one piece.

NOTES

Chapter 3:
Home-Wreckers Need Fathers

Blaze, John. "The Power of Fathers." Focus on the Family. Accessed 2008.

http://www.focusonthefamily.com/parenting/parenting-roles/the-power-of-fathers/the-power-of-fathers#_ga=1.41016098.1057762282.1475188047.

Gregorie, Sheila Wray. "How Technology Threatens Marriages - To Love, Honor and Vacuum." To Love Honor and Vacuum. April 5, 2013. Accessed April 5, 2013. http://tolovehonorandvacuum.com/2013/04/how-technology-threatens-marriages/.

Keller, Timothy, Kathy Keller, Spence Shelton, Jeff White, TJ Rathburn, Mai Hairu-Powell, and Scott Kauffmann. *The Meaning of Marriage Study Guide.: A Vision for Married and Single People.*

Lindsey, Michelle. "Follow Your Heart (and Other Bad Ideas)." Nitty Gritty Love. August 11, 2013. Accessed August 11, 2013. http://www.nittygrittylove.com/follow-your-heart-and-other-bad-ideas/.

Chapter 4:
The Blame Game

Laaser, Debra. *Shattered Vows: Hope and Healing for Women Who Have Been Sexually Betrayed*. Grand Rapids, MI: Zondervan, 2008.

Chapter 5:
When in Limbo

Dobson, James C. *Love Must Be Tough*. Sisters, Or.: Multnomah, 2003.

Chapter 9:
For the Jesus Folk

Holy Bible: New Living Translation. Wheaton, IL: Tyndale House Publishers, 2004.

Lewis, C. S. *The Screwtape Letters.* Philadelphia: Fortress Press, 1980.

Lewis, C. S. *Mere Christianity: A Revised and Amplified Edition, with a New Introduction, of the Three Books, Broadcast Talks, Christian Behaviour, and Beyond Personality.* San Francisco: HarperSanFrancisco, 2001.

Chapter 10:
The D Word

Grissom, Steve, and Kathy Leonard. *DivorceCare: Hope, Help, and Healing during and after Your Divorce.* Nashville, TN: Nelson Books, 2005.